D1379038

# cats

## the ultimate cat lover's guide

Catherine Davidson

igloobooks

Published in 2013
by Igloo Books Ltd
Cottage Farm
Sywell
NN6 0BJ
www.igloobooks.com

SHE001 0913
2 4 6 8 10 9 7 5 3 1
ISBN: 978-1-78197-889-4

Photo Acknowledgements

Istock/Susana Machado, 11; Alamy/Graham Ella, 14; Istock/Stefan Hermans, 12; Istock/Eric Isselée, 25, 75, and
167; Istock/Ina Peters 26; Getty/Dorling Kindersley, 27; Istock/Igor Grochev, 29; Istock/Vladimir Suponev, 37; Istock/
Cathrine Scott, 55; Getty/Steve Gorton and Tim Ridley, 87; Istock/Florea Marius Catalin, 88; Istock/Mehmet Salin
Gutler, 89; Istock/Justin Horrocks, 99; Alamy/ H. Reinhard, 100 and 101; Istock/Erik Lam, 121; Istock/Slarvomir
Jastrzebski, 131; Istock/Robyn Glover, 155; Istock/Photos.com, 161; Alamy/Yann Arthus-Bertrand, 168; Istock/
Nikolay Titov, 173; Alamy/Alan Robinson, 175; and Marc Henrie 13, 15, 16, 17, 19, 21, 22, 23, 31, 33, 35, 39, 40, 41,
42, 43, 44, 45, 46, 47, 48, 49, 50, 51, 53, 57, 59, 60, 61, 62, 63, 64, 65, 67, 69, 71, 73, 77, 83, 84, 88, 90, 91, 93, 95,
96, 97, 98, 102, 103, 105, 107, 111, 113, 115, 117, 119, 123, 125, 127, 129, 133, 135, 139, 141, 142, 143, 144, 146,
149, 151, 153, 155, 157, 159, 163, 165, and 171.

Igloo Books would like to thank Donna Cox for her description of the Pixie Bob on pages 162 and 163 and
permission to use the image of her cat, Grand Champion Alsoomse Red Cloud at Sundown, Aka Solo.

Printed and manufactured in China

# cats

## the ultimate cat lover's guide

# Contents

# Introduction

Every breed of cat has its own distinct and special charm. Some cats are supremely elegant, others have luxuriant fur seemingly designed for stroking, yet others are blessed with playful personalities that endear them to young and old alike. Whatever kind of feline companion you are looking for, you will find it among the hundred beautiful cats featured in this book.

The way your cat looks is an essential part of its appeal. But before you welcome a cat into your home, it is important that you consider its character and its physical requirements, too. That way you can be sure that you pick the right cat for you and your lifestyle—and of giving your chosen cat everything it needs for a happy life.

Each breed has its own personality: consider whether you would get on best with a sociable and affectionate animal, such as the Tonkinese, or whether you want a sedate lap cat, such as the Ragdoll.

Some cats are self-contained enough to amuse themselves when you are not there. Others — such as the attention-seeking Siamese —cannot tolerate being left alone. If you have children, dogs, or other animals, then you will obviously need to choose a cat that can get along with them.

Equally, you should think about whether you need a cat that will be happy to spend its time within the confines of your home, or whether you can give it safe access to outdoors. Most cats can adapt to an indoor life, but some need planty of outdoor space in which to roam and hunt. There are grooming requirements to consider, too. Many breeds, especially the shorthairs, need little care in order to maintain their coats. Longhaired cats, with their beautifully thick coats, naturally require more regular—sometimes daily—grooming. Be realistic: caring for a longhaired cat takes a great deal of time and effort, and you need to be sure that you can commit to this before making your choice.

Whichever cat you decide on, you should be

sure to buy it from a reputable breeder, who will give you precise instructions on how best to care for it. You should give thought to the ongoing costs of owning a cat: innoculations, neutering or spaying, unexpected vet's fees if your cat becomes ill, and so on.

## Pedigree cats

Each of the cats featured in this book is described in detail, to help you decide whether it is the right cat for you. The standards cited are those set by the major cat associations. These include the British Governing Council of the Cat Fancy (GCCF), the American Cat Fanciers' Association (CFA), TICA (The International Cat Association), and the European Fédération Internationale Féline (FIFé).

Cat associations have differing rules and definitions, so a particular cat may be considered a color variation of one breed in one country, and an entirely separate breed elsewhere. Sometimes the same breed will be known by different names, and often breeds that are accepted by one association may not be recognized at all by another. Where possible, these differences are covered in the relevant cat profile.

It is important to remember that the cat association standards are ideals used for judging show cats. Your own cat may fall short of the breed standard in one way or another, but it is still likely to be a beautiful cat that displays the distinctive traits of its breed.

Non-pedigree cats—known as moggies—are further removed from the pedigree standard, but they too make wonderful family cats.

Whatever cat you choose, you can look forward to long years of feline companionship. Cats can live up to 18 years, and so to own a cat means to enrich your life over a long period. So long as you choose wisely, it is a commitment that you are unlikely ever to regret.

A thumbnail sketch of each breed, covering its physique, the color of its coat, its temperament, and its grooming needs.

An at-a-glance guide to key facts about the breed: its size, coat care requirements, activeness, friendliness, and playfulness. One paw print means it is at the lesser end of the scale: for example, that it is a relatively small cat or that its coat is easy to groom. Four paw prints mean that it is at the upper end: for example, that it is exceptionally friendly or playful.

An insight into the story behind the breed, and a description of the defining characteristics.

Brief portraits of all the main features of the breed, according to the breed standards set by the cat associations.

# Shorthaired Cats

Most cats have short coats, like the wild cats from which they are descended. A short coat is highly practical: it is unlikely to become tangled, and it offers protection against injury. From an owner's point of view, it requires minimal grooming. Shorthaired cats fall into two basic types. On the one hand, there is the sturdy, compact cat typified by the British or American Shorthair. On the other hand, there are the foreign or Oriental cats—such as the Siamese—which are slim and long-bodied.

# Black British Shorthair

## BLACK BRITISH SHORTHAIR FACTS

**PHYSIQUE** A large, broad-chested cat with a compact muscular body and sturdy, stocky legs—the build is described as "cobby."

**COAT** Black is one of the widely accepted self (solid) colors for the British Shorthair breed. The coat must not have any white hairs, brown tinge or other markings.

**TEMPERAMENT** This is an adaptable and affectionate cat with a calm disposition. As befits its street origins, it is a good hunter.

**GROOMING** Occasional brushing will keep this cat's coat shiny and in good condition.

The Black British Shorthair is the pedigree version of the black cat of folklore. For centuries, black cats were maligned as the familiars of witches or agents of the devil, and to this day they remain the subject of many superstitions.
But the innate appeal of the jet-black coat has always been recognized, and was carefully fostered by the first British breeders.

The British Shorthair is the national British cat, although it is probably derived from cats brought to Britain by the Romans in the first century AD. Through the centuries that followed, this working cat became an integral part of the everyday scene in Britain. This is evidenced by the presence of the animal in folktales and verses ("Pussycat, pussycat, where have you been…?"), in English lore ("If a black cat crosses your path…"), and in the English language ("Cat got your tongue?").

In Victorian times, the best exemplars of Britain's street cats and farm cats were selectively bred to create pedigree animals.
The Black was recognized from the start, and was among the contenders at Britain's first cat show at London's Crystal Palace in 1871.
The British Shorthair breed as a whole went into sharp decline at the beginning of the 20th century, and it was only after the Second World War that fans of this archetypal British cat managed to revive its fortunes. Today, the British Shorthair is the most popular breed in its native Britain. Nevertheless, this breed has remained comparatively rare outside its homeland. It was not officially recognized in the United States until 1980—over 100 years after its first appearance.

The British Shorthair is a strong and sturdy cat, good at hunting but with a reserved and loyal nature. The male of the species is considerably larger than the female; and, curiously, four in ten Shorthairs have blood of the rare Type B. All the Shorthairs except for the White and the Colorpointed have vibrant golden or coppery eyes. This feature is particularly attractive in the Black, whose eyes are like two golden rings on a jeweller's black baize.

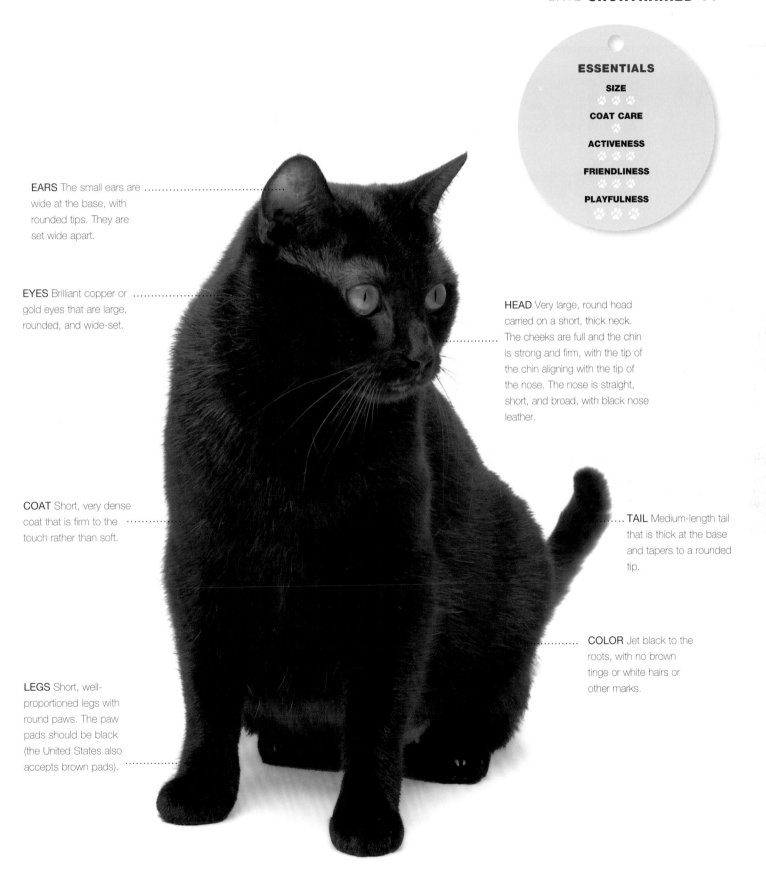

**ESSENTIALS**

SIZE

COAT CARE

ACTIVENESS

FRIENDLINESS

PLAYFULNESS

**EARS** The small ears are wide at the base, with rounded tips. They are set wide apart.

**EYES** Brilliant copper or gold eyes that are large, rounded, and wide-set.

**COAT** Short, very dense coat that is firm to the touch rather than soft.

**LEGS** Short, well-proportioned legs with round paws. The paw pads should be black (the United States also accepts brown pads).

**HEAD** Very large, round head carried on a short, thick neck. The cheeks are full and the chin is strong and firm, with the tip of the chin aligning with the tip of the nose. The nose is straight, short, and broad, with black nose leather.

**TAIL** Medium-length tail that is thick at the base and tapers to a rounded tip.

**COLOR** Jet black to the roots, with no brown tinge or white hairs or other marks.

# Blue British Shorthair

## BLUE BRITISH SHORTHAIR FACTS

**PHYSIQUE** A large, broad-chested cat with a compact muscular body and sturdy, stocky legs—the build is described as "cobby."

**COAT** Blue British Shorthairs have a light to medium blue coat, without shadings, white hairs, or other markings.

**TEMPERAMENT** This is an adaptable and affectionate cat with a calm disposition. As befits its street origins, it is a good hunter.

**GROOMING** Occasional brushing will keep this cat's blue coat shiny and in good condition.

For many, this cat epitomizes the best of the British Shorthairs. Blue was one of the earliest colors to be bred, and the breed as a whole was once known as the "British Blue." At one time, blue was the only color to be recognized in the United States, and it is the most popular of all the British Shorthair colors.

**HEAD** Very large, round head carried on a short, thick neck. The cheeks are full and the chin is strong and firm, with the tip of the chin aligning with the tip of the nose. The nose is straight, short, and broad, with blue nose leather.

**COLOR** Light to medium blue, with no tabby marking, white hairs, or silver tipping.

**TAIL** Medium-length tail that is thick at the base and tapers to a rounded tip.

**EARS** The small ears are wide at the base, with rounded tips. They are set wide apart.

**EYES** Brilliant copper or gold eyes that are large, rounded, and wide-set.

**COAT** Short, very dense coat that is firm to the touch rather than soft.

**LEGS** Short, well-proportioned legs with round paws. The paw pads should be blue.

### ESSENTIALS

SIZE

COAT CARE

ACTIVENESS

FRIENDLINESS

PLAYFULNESS

# White British Shorthair

White cats have always been esteemed for their pristine coats. The White British Shorthair has been bred since the late 1800s, but remains uncommon. Eye color can vary: the cat can be blue-eyed, orange-eyed, or have one eye of each color. The blue-eyed and the odd-eyed varieties are prone to deafness, so orange-eyed cats are now most often seen.

## WHITE BRITISH SHORTHAIR FACTS

**PHYSIQUE** A large, broad-chested cat with a compact muscular body and sturdy, stocky legs—the build is described as "cobby."

**COAT** White is one of the widely accepted self (solid) colors for the British Shorthair. The coat must not have a yellow tinge.

**TEMPERAMENT** This is an adaptable and affectionate cat with a calm disposition. As befits its street origins, it is a good hunter.

**GROOMING** Occasional brushing will keep this cat's white coat in good condition.

**COAT** Short, very dense coat that is firm to the touch rather than soft.

**EARS** The small ears are wide at the base with rounded tips. They are set wide apart.

**EYES** The eyes may be bright sapphire blue, brilliant copper, or gold, or the cat may have one eye that is blue and one that is copper or gold. They are large, rounded, and wide-set.

**TAIL** Medium-length tail that is thick at the base and tapers to a rounded tip.

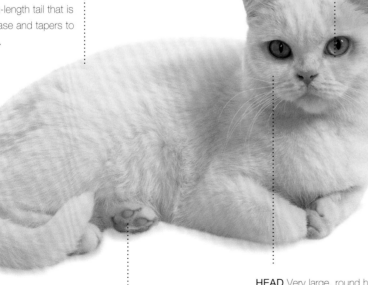

**COLOR** Pure white with no yellow tinge.

**LEGS** Short, well-proportioned legs with round paws. The paw pads should be pink.

**HEAD** Very large, round head carried on a short, thick neck. The cheeks are full and the chin is strong and firm, with the tip of the chin aligning with the tip of the nose. The nose is straight, short, and broad, with pink nose leather.

**ESSENTIALS**

SIZE

COAT CARE

ACTIVENESS

FRIENDLINESS

PLAYFULNESS

# Cream British Shorthair

## CREAM BRITISH SHORTHAIR FACTS

🐾 **PHYSIQUE** A large, broad-chested cat with a compact muscular body and sturdy, stocky legs—the build is described as "cobby."

🐾 **COAT** The Cream British Shorthair has a rich cream coat that is a paler version of the Red British Shorthair.

🐾 **TEMPERAMENT** This is an adaptable and affectionate cat with a calm disposition. As befits its street origins, it is a good hunter.

🐾 **GROOMING** Occasional brushing is all that is needed to keep this cat's cream coat in good condition.

The Cream British Shorthair is a dilute version of the Red. Both varieties are hard to breed without tabby markings and, as a result, they became established as pedigree breeds later than other self, or solid, colors, such as the black or the blue. The Cream was officially recognized in the UK in the 1920s.

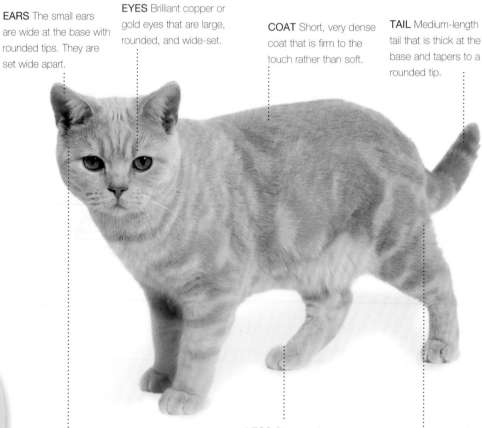

**EARS** The small ears are wide at the base with rounded tips. They are set wide apart.

**EYES** Brilliant copper or gold eyes that are large, rounded, and wide-set.

**COAT** Short, very dense coat that is firm to the touch rather than soft.

**TAIL** Medium-length tail that is thick at the base and tapers to a rounded tip.

**HEAD** Very large, round head carried on a short, thick neck. The cheeks are full and the chin is strong and firm, with the tip of the chin aligning with the tip of the nose. The nose is straight, short, and broad, with pink nose leather that may be slightly freckled.

**LEGS** Short, well-proportioned legs with round paws. The paw pads should be pink and may be slightly freckled.

**COLOR** Pale cream to the roots with no white hairs. Ideally, the cat will have no tabby markings.

## ESSENTIALS

**SIZE**
🐾 🐾 🐾

**COAT CARE**
🐾

**ACTIVENESS**
🐾 🐾 🐾

**FRIENDLINESS**
🐾 🐾 🐾

**PLAYFULNESS**
🐾 🐾 🐾 🐾

# Chocolate British Shorthair

The Chocolate is one of the more novel colors to be seen among British Shorthairs. Breeders are always looking to create new and unusual varieties of British Shorthair. The Chocolate, with its warm cocoa-colored fur, is the result of outcrossing with the Himalayan (Colorpoint Persian). It is not yet universally accepted outside the United Kingdom.

## CHOCOLATE BRITISH SHORTHAIR FACTS

**PHYSIQUE** A large, broad-chested cat with a compact muscular body and sturdy, stocky legs—the build is commonly described as "cobby."

**COAT** Chocolate is one of the typically Eastern self (solid) colors introduced; others include lilac, cinnamon, and fawn. They are not recognized in the United States.

**TEMPERAMENT** This is an adaptable and affectionate cat with a calm and loyal disposition. As befits its street origins, it is a good hunter.

**GROOMING** Occasional brushing is advised to keep this cat's chocolate coat in good condition.

**EARS** The small ears are wide at the base with rounded tips. They are set wide apart.

**EYES** Brilliant copper or gold eyes that are large, rounded, and wide-set.

**HEAD** Very large, round head carried on a short, thick neck. The cheeks are full and the chin is strong and firm, with the tip of the chin aligning with the tip of the nose. The nose is straight, short, and broad, with chocolate or pink nose leather.

**LEGS** Short, well-proportioned legs with round paws. The paw pads should be chocolate or pink.

**COLOR** The coat is a rich chocolate-brown that extends to the roots, with no white hairs.

**COAT** Short, very dense coat that is firm to the touch rather than soft.

**TAIL** Medium-length tail that is thick at the base and tapers to a rounded tip.

## ESSENTIALS

SIZE

COAT CARE

ACTIVENESS

FRIENDLINESS

PLAYFULNESS

# Lilac British Shorthair

## LILAC BRITISH SHORTHAIR FACTS

**PHYSIQUE** A large, broad-chested cat with a compact muscular body and sturdy, stocky legs—the build is often described as "cobby.'"

**COAT** Lilac is one of the Eastern self colors to be introduced; others include chocolate, cinnamon, and fawn. They are not recognized in the United States.

**TEMPERAMENT** This is an adaptable and affectionate cat with a calm and loyal disposition. As befits its street origins, it is a good hunter.

**GROOMING** Occasional brushing is advised to keep this cat's lilac coat in good condition.

The Lilac originated in the UK and is a dilute version of the Chocolate. This cat's fur is a delightful frosty gray with a pinkish tone—which is quite distinct from the blue-gray coat of the Blue. The American Cat Fanciers' Association does not recognize the Lilac or Chocolate, but both are accepted by other registries.

**EARS** The small ears are wide at the base with rounded tips. They are set wide apart.

**HEAD** Large, round head on a short, thick neck. The cheeks are full, with a strong, firm chin—its tip aligns with the tip of the nose, whch is straight, short, and broad, with pinkish lilac nose leather.

**COLOR** The coat is a pinkish gray, which extends to the roots, with no white hairs.

**EYES** Brilliant copper or gold eyes that are large, rounded, and wide-set.

**COAT** Short, very dense coat that is firm to the touch rather than soft.

**LEGS** Short, well-proportioned legs with round paws. The paw pads should be pinkish lilac.

**TAIL** Medium-length tail that is thick at the base and tapers to a rounded tip.

**ESSENTIALS**

SIZE

COAT CARE

ACTIVENESS

FRIENDLINESS

PLAYFULNESS

# Bicolor British Shorthair

Bicolored cats are often seen on the streets, but perfect pedigree specimens are far less common. This is because there are stringent standards for the amount of white that is deemed permissible in a pedigree bicolor. Moreover, the patches of color should ideally be well balanced and symmetrical—something that is difficult to achieve.

**COAT** Short, very dense coat that is firm to the touch rather than soft.

**EYES** Brilliant copper or gold eyes that are large, rounded, and wide-set.

**EARS** The small ears are wide at the base with rounded tips. They are set wide apart.

**TAIL** Medium-length tail that is thick at the base and tapers to a rounded tip.

**LEGS** Short, well-proportioned legs with round paws. The paw pads should be pink or harmonize with the colored parts.

**COLOR** In the UK standard, the white should cover at least one-third and no more than half of the body. The American standard calls for some white on the feet, legs, undersides, chest, and muzzle. The patches of color should be symmetrical.

**HEAD** Very large, round head carried on a short, thick neck. The cheeks are full and the chin is strong and firm, with the tip of the chin aligning with the tip of the nose. The nose is straight, short, and broad, with nose leather that is pink or harmonizes with the coat color.

## BICOLOR BRITISH SHORTHAIR FACTS

**PHYSIQUE** A large, broad-chested cat with a compact muscular body and sturdy, stocky legs—the build is often described as "cobby."

**COAT** Bicolors are a mixture of white and any of the recognized self (solid) and tortoiseshell colors. In the Van Bicolor, the colored parts are restricted to the head, tail, and legs.

**TEMPERAMENT** This is an adaptable and affectionate cat with a calm disposition. As befits its street origins, it is a good hunter.

**GROOMING** Occasional brushing is advised to maintain the coat in good condition.

### ESSENTIALS

**SIZE**

**COAT CARE**

**ACTIVENESS**

**FRIENDLINESS**

**PLAYFULNESS**

# Tabby British Shorthair

## TABBY BRITISH SHORTHAIR FACTS

**PHYSIQUE** A large, broad-chested cat with a compact muscular body and sturdy, stocky legs—the build is often described as "cobby."

**COAT** The tabby comes in three coat patterns: classic, mackerel, and spotted. The traditional colors are red, blue, brown, and cream, but chocolate and lilac are also accepted, except in the United States. There are also silver versions of all the colors.

**TEMPERAMENT** This is an adaptable and affectionate cat with a calm disposition. As befits its street ancestry, it is a good hunter.

**GROOMING** Occasional brushing will keep the tabby coat in good condition.

The tabby pattern is, in effect, a form of camouflage. As such, it represents a visible link between domestic cats and their wild ancestors. The tabby gene is strong, and faint tabby markings are often discernible on non-tabby breeds. In a perfect pedigree Tabby British Shorthair, the tabby markings form a distinctive and balanced pattern on the cat's body.

The Tabby comes in three coat patterns; classic, mackerel, and spotted, and is accepted in many colours. The traditional colors are red, blue, brown and cream but chocolate and lilac are also accepted (except in the US). There are also silver versions of all the colors.

This breed is highly popular in Britain, its native land – although it probably derived from specimens brought over by the Romans in the first century AD. The endearing qualities of this cat are its round features; the head is rounded with full cheeks and a thick neck; the eyes are large, round and wide set; even the belly is quite round – these cats do enjoy eating! They are very gentles creatures who enjoy affection, and are irresistibly cuddly.

Extremely friendly and playful, The British Shorthair makes an excellent family pet due to its loving temperament. Although a very affectionate cat, this breed may opt to keep out of the way of younger children if they are not as gentle as other humans. Generally a healthy breed, these cats have a good lifespan, sometimes up to fifteen years, and make reliable companions for life. A dignified and intelligent cat, The Tabby British Shorthair is a common sight around Britain and is a thriving breed.

**ESSENTIALS**

SIZE

COAT CARE

ACTIVENESS

FRIENDLINESS

PLAYFULNESS

**HEAD** Very large, round head carried on a short, thick neck. The cheeks are full and the chin is strong and firm, with the tip of the chin aligning with the tip of the nose. The nose is straight, short, and broad with nose leather that complements the coat.

**EYES** The eyes are large, rounded, and wide-set. Brilliant copper or gold eyes are desirable but colors may vary.

**EARS** The small ears are wide at the base with rounded tips. They are set wide apart.

**COAT** Short, very dense coat that is firm to the touch rather than soft.

**TAIL** Medium-length tail that is thick at the base and tapers to a rounded tip.

**LEGS** Short, well-proportioned legs with round paws. The paw pads should complement the main coat color.

**COLOR** In the mackerel tabby pattern, parallel stripes run down the spine, forming a narrow saddle. In the classic, the spine stripes are well separated and there is an oyster-shaped swirl surrounding a blotch on each flank. The spotted has a spotted body, but often striped legs and tail.

# Tortoiseshell British Shorthair

## TORTOISESHELL BRITISH SHORTHAIR FACTS

**PHYSIQUE** A large broad-chested cat with a compact muscular body and sturdy, stocky legs—the build is often described as "cobby."

**COAT** As well as the black, red, and cream tortie, there are blue-cream, chocolate, and lilac varieties. Only the Tortie and Blue-Cream are recognized in the United States.

**TEMPERAMENT** This is an adaptable and affectionate cat with a calm and loyal disposition. As befits its street ancestry, it is a good hunter.

**GROOMING** Occasional brushing will keep the tortoiseshell's coat in good condition.

The classic tortoiseshell—"Tortie" for short—has a coat of black, red, and cream. The colors should be softly intermingled, with no obvious patches; there may be a narrow blaze on the face. For genetic reasons, almost all tortoiseshells are female. They are difficult to breed, but were among the first British Shorthairs to be shown.

The coat of the British Tortoiseshell is one of the most familiar and desired patterns of all domestic cats, yet cats with this coloring are surprisingly difficult to breed. The distinctive patches of black, cream and red are best achieved by breeding a queen with a solid-colored black, red or cream male. Even with the pairing the litter may only contain one kitten with the desired colouring, which – due to the genes that determine colour – is almost always female.

There are two variations of Tortoiseshell; the first being a tortoiseshell and white variety which differs only because of the splashes of white that appear amidst the traditional 'tortie' coloring. The second is a blue tortoiseshell and white variety in which the black is replaced by blue and the red is replaced by cream – this is known as Dulite Calico in the US. The British Tortoiseshell is an affectionate cat that has been a wonderful and highly popular pet for years. Originally bred from the best street cats, this breed is a good hunter like many shorthairs. It has a strong and muscular body, with short but proportionate legs and a short, thick tail. A calm cat, the Tortoiseshell is adaptable and sharp-witted and is often described as a charming companion.

**EYES** Brilliant copper or gold eyes that are large, rounded, and wide-set.

**EARS** The small ears are wide at the base with rounded tips. They are set wide apart.

**ESSENTIALS**

SIZE

COAT CARE

ACTIVENESS

FRIENDLINESS

PLAYFULNESS

**HEAD** Very large, round head carried on a short, thick neck. The cheeks are full and the chin is strong and firm, with the tip of the chin aligning with the tip of the nose. The nose is straight, short, and broad with nose leather that complements the base color of the coat.

**COAT** Short, very dense coat that is firm to the touch rather than soft.

**COLOR** The colors are evenly mingled all over rather than patched. There should be no tabby markings.

**LEGS** Short, well-proportioned legs with round paws. The paw pads should complement the base color of the coat.

**TAIL** Medium-length tail that is thick at the base and tapers to a rounded tip.

# Colorpointed British Shorthair

## COLORPOINTED BRITISH SHORTHAIR FACTS

**PHYSIQUE** A large, broad-chested cat with a compact muscular body and sturdy, stocky legs—the build is described as "cobby."

**COAT** The Colorpointed is recognized in the following colors: seal, blue, chocolate, lilac, red, cream, cinnamon, and fawn. There are also tortie, tabby, and smoke varieties.

**TEMPERAMENT** This is an adaptable and affectionate cat with a calm disposition. As befits its street origins, it is a good hunter.

**GROOMING** Occasional brushing will keep this cat's coat in good condition.

The Colorpointed British Shorthair has the delicate coloring and brilliant blue eyes of a Siamese. Its coat pattern—a pale body with darker points—was achieved by outcrossing with the Himalayan (Colorpoint Longhair), which has a cobby body shape similar to the British Shorthair. The Colorpointed British Shorthair is still rare in Britain, and it is not recognized in the United States.

**COLOR** The body is pale with dark ears, mask, tail, and legs. Any shading should tone with the color of the points.

**EARS** The small ears are wide at the base with rounded tips. They are set wide apart.

**EYES** Clear blue eyes that are large, rounded, and wide-set.

**COAT** Short, very dense coat that is firm to the touch rather than soft.

**ESSENTIALS**

SIZE

COAT CARE

ACTIVENESS

FRIENDLINESS

PLAYFULNESS

**TAIL** Medium-length tail that is thick at the base and tapers to a rounded tip.

**HEAD** Very large, round head carried on a short, thick neck. The cheeks are full and the chin is strong and firm, with the tip of the chin aligning with the tip of the nose. The nose is straight, short, and broad, with nose leather that complements the color of the points.

**LEGS** Short, well-proportioned legs with round paws. The paw pads should complement the color of the points.

# Tipped British Shorthair

The handsome Tipped British Shorthair has a pale undercoat and a topcoat delicately tipped with black. The pattern creates a shimmering effect when the cat moves. There is also a Smoke British Shorthair in which the darker color extends so far down the hair that the pale undercoat is revealed only when the cat is in motion.

**LEGS** Short, well-proportioned legs with round paws. The paw pads should correspond to the coat color (they may be mottled in tortie varieties).

**EYES** The eyes are large, rounded, and wide-set. They are green in the black-tipped cat, copper or orange in other colors, and have a dark outline.

**EARS** The small ears are wide at the base with rounded tips. They are set wide apart.

**TAIL** Medium-length tail that is thick at the base and tapers to a rounded tip.

**HEAD** Large, round head carried on a short, thick neck. The cheeks are full and the chin is strong, with the tip of the chin aligning with the tip of the nose. The nose is straight, short, and broad, with nose leather that is brick red or corresponds to the coat color.

**COAT** Short, very dense coat that is firm to the touch rather than soft.

**COLOR** The undercoat is so pale that it appears white, and the topcoat is tipped with color on the back, flanks, head, ears, and tail. The tipping should be even.

## TIPPED BRITISH SHORTHAIR FACTS

**PHYSIQUE** A large, broad-chested cat with a compact, muscular body and sturdy, stocky legs.

**COAT** The Tipped, like the Smoke, comes in all recognized self (solid) and tortie colors. There is a golden version with an apricot rather than pale undercoat. In the United States, tipped cats are called Shaded Silver, or Chinchilla Silver for the most lightly tipped version; there are also gold and red varieties.

**TEMPERAMENT** An adaptable, affectionate cat with a calm disposition.

**GROOMING** Occasional brushing is advised to keep the coat in good condition.

### ESSENTIALS

**SIZE**
🐾🐾🐾

**COAT CARE**
🐾

**ACTIVENESS**
🐾🐾🐾

**FRIENDLINESS**
🐾🐾🐾

**PLAYFULNESS**
🐾🐾🐾

# Tabby American Shorthair

## TABBY AMERICAN SHORTHAIR FACTS

**PHYSIQUE** Medium to large cat with a powerful body, well-developed shoulders, and muscular legs.

**COAT** The American Shorthair comes in many colors and patterns. Both classic and mackerel tabby patterns are accepted in the following colors: red, brown, blue, silver, blue-silver, and cameo. There is also a patched tabby (tabby with additional patches of red or cream) in silver, brown, blue, and blue-silver.

**TEMPERAMENT** This is an active and outgoing cat that makes an affectionate pet. They are also good hunters.

**GROOMING** Occasional brushing is advised to keep the coat in good condition.

It is sometimes said that the ancestors of the American Shorthair sailed with the *Mayflower*. It is not known whether a cat came ashore at Plymouth Rock, but certainly many European settlers brought rat-hunters with them to North America. In the United States, they evolved into the lithe, tough breed we now know as the American Shorthair, with the Tabby proving the most popular.

The American domestic cat took a different path from its British cousin. As it spread across the continent with the pioneers, it faced more natural predators and a harsher climate than its forebears. Smaller, weaker specimens tended not to survive, and so by a process of natural selection, the American house-cat grew large and strong. It evolved a thick, hard coat that kept it warm and afforded some protection from injury.

The essential characteristics of the American Shorthair were therefore already in place when, towards the end of the 19th century, breeders began to show an interest. But the first "Domestic Shorthairs," as they were known, were not seen as an important breed. That changed in 1896, when a price of US$2,500 was placed on a brown Tabby Domestic Shorthair exhibited at the Second Annual Cat Show at Madison Square Garden, New York. Shorthairs were in vogue, and at the turn of the century an orange tabby (albeit one imported from Britain) became the first Domestic Shorthair to be registered as a pedigree cat in the United States. In 1904, the same owner registered a male smoke named Buster Brown—the first American-born Domestic Shorthair.

By the 1950s, the breed was well established at shows across the continent. But somehow it still suffered from a certain lack of status. Again, it took a tabby to change the situation. In 1965, a silver specimen named Shawnee Trademark was awarded the title "Cat of the Year" by the American Cat Fanciers' Association. This accolade speeded the acceptance of a new and more prestigious name for the breed in general: the American Shorthair, which now comes in as many as 100 different varieties.

**ESSENTIALS**

SIZE

COAT CARE

ACTIVENESS

FRIENDLINESS

PLAYFULNESS

**EYES** Large, rounded eyes that are wide-set and slightly slanted. The color is gold or green.

**COLOR** In the mackerel tabby pattern, parallel stripes run down the spine, forming a narrow saddle. In the classic tabby pattern, the spine stripes are well separated and there is an oyster-shaped swirl surrounding a blotch on each flank. The patched tabby has additional patches of red or cream.

**EARS** Medium-sized with slightly rounded tips.

**HEAD** Large head with full cheeks and squarish muzzle, set on a medium-length, strong neck. The nose is medium in length and the nose leather complements the coat. The tip of the nose aligns vertically with the tip of the chin.

**TAIL** Medium-long tail with a thick base and blunt tip.

**COAT** Short, dense coat that feels firm rather than soft to the touch.

**LEGS** Medium-length, powerful legs.

**PAWS** Heavy, rounded paws with pads that complement the coat.

# Bicolor American Shorthair

## BICOLOR AMERICAN SHORTHAIR FACTS

**PHYSIQUE** A medium to large cat with a powerful body, well-developed shoulders, and muscular legs. Male cats are significantly larger than the females.

**COAT** The Bicolor and Van Bicolor come in black, blue, red, or cream. There are also tortoiseshell and dilute tortoiseshell varieties—the Calico and Dilute Calico.

**TEMPERAMENT** An active and outgoing cat that makes an affectionate pet. American Shorthairs are good hunters.

**GROOMING** Occasional brushing is advised to maintain the coat.

The ideal Bicolor is a cat of clear contrasts that exhibits well-defined patches of black, blue, red, or cream. In a perfect show speciman the feet, legs, underside, chest, and muzzle should all be pure white. In the Van Bicolor the patches are confined to the head, tail, and legs—in the manner of the distinctly patterned Turkish Van.

**EARS** Medium-sized with slightly rounded tips.

**EYES** Large, rounded eyes that are wide-set and slightly slanted. The color is brilliant gold.

**HEAD** Large head with full cheeks and squarish muzzle, set on a medium-length, strong neck. The nose is medium in length and the nose leather harmonizes with the colored parts. The tip of the nose aligns vertically with the tip of the chin.

**COAT** Short, dense coat that feels firm rather than soft to the touch.

**COLOR** In the Bicolor there should be well-defined patches of color on the body. The feet, legs, undersides, chests, and muzzle should be white.

**LEGS** Medium-length, powerful legs.

**PAWS** Heavy, rounded paws with pads that harmonize with the colored parts.

**TAIL** Medium-long tail with a thick base and blunt tip.

### ESSENTIALS

SIZE

COAT CARE

ACTIVENESS

FRIENDLINESS

PLAYFULNESS

# Calico American Shorthair

The appealing tortoiseshell-and-white American Shorthair is known as the "Calico" cat throughout North America. The name refers to the bold patterning of the coat, which is reminiscent of the variegated designs that used to be printed on calico fabric. The Calico American Shorthair name has been used since the first cat shows at the end of the 19th century.

**HEAD** Large head with full cheeks and squarish muzzle, set on a medium-length, strong neck. A medium-length nose; the nose leather complements the colored parts. The tip of the nose aligns vertically with the tip of the chin.

**TAIL** Medium-long tail with a thick base and blunt tip.

**COAT** Short, dense coat that feels firm rather than soft to the touch.

**EARS** Medium-sized with slightly rounded tips.

**EYES** Large, rounded eyes that are wide-set and slightly slanted. The color is brilliant gold in the adult cat, though the kitten does not show full eye color.

**LEGS** Medium-length, powerful legs.

**PAWS** Heavy, rounded paws with pads that harmonize with the colored parts.

**COLOR** Clearly defined patches of color on a white body.

## CALICO AMERICAN SHORTHAIR FACTS

**PHYSIQUE** A medium to large cat with a powerful body, well-developed shoulders, and muscular legs. Male cats are significantly larger than the females.

**COAT** The Calico is a white cat with black and red patches. There is also a Dilute Calico, with patches of blue and cream.

**TEMPERAMENT** An active and outgoing cat that makes an affectionate pet, these cats are good hunters.

**GROOMING** Occasional brushing is advised to maintain the condition of the coat.

### ESSENTIALS

**SIZE**

**COAT CARE**

**ACTIVENESS**

**FRIENDLINESS**

**PLAYFULNESS**

# European Shorthair

## EUROPEAN SHORTHAIR FACTS

**PHYSIQUE** Medium to large, well-muscled body that is not as cobby as the British Shorthair. The chest is broad and the legs are sturdy, giving the overall impression of a strong, robust cat.

**COAT** The European Shorthair comes in white, black, blue, red, and cream self (solid) colors. There are also tortie, smoke, tabby, silver tabby, bicolor, and van bicolor varieties.

**TEMPERAMENT** This is an affectionate, calm, and independent cat that needs plenty of outdoor time. The European Shorthair is a prolific breeder.

**GROOMING** Regular brushing will keep the coat in good condition.

The European Shorthair is the European equivalent of the British Shorthair and the American Shorthair, but is physically different from both. Although there have been shorthaired cats in Europe for thousands of years, the European Shorthair as a pedigree breed is a newcomer, and as such, it is still not recognized by most British and American registries.

For many years, no distinction was drawn between the domestic cats of mainland Europe and those in the UK. They were seen as essentially the same breed, and the standard for pedigree cats was the one laid down by the British General Council of Cat Fanciers. This situation began to change after the Second World War, when Sweden made it possible for breeders to register shorthaired cats.

This was the first step towards establishing the European domestic cat as a breed in its own right. It was also noted in the postwar years that the best examples of European cats tended to be less cobby and more muscular than the British norm; they were also generally larger than the American cat, and thinner in the face. These traits were perhaps a reflection of the warm, Mediterranean climate in which many European cats developed.

In 1982, the Federation Internationale Féline (FIFé), the main European registry, recognized the European Shorthair as a breed with its own standard. This gave European breeders a type to aim for, and encouraged the divergence of the European Shorthair from its British counterpart—all the more so since crosses with British Shorthairs are not permitted in the pedigree.

The effect of FIFé's ruling was to create a readymade breed, because there were already plenty of good European cats in all possible colors and patterns. FIFé also granted the European Shorthair "open registration" at shows, meaning that any cat could compete, as long as it conformed to a certain standard. This policy tended to bring forth the finest specimens, which could then be used to widen the gene pool of the European Shorthair and so strengthen the breed.

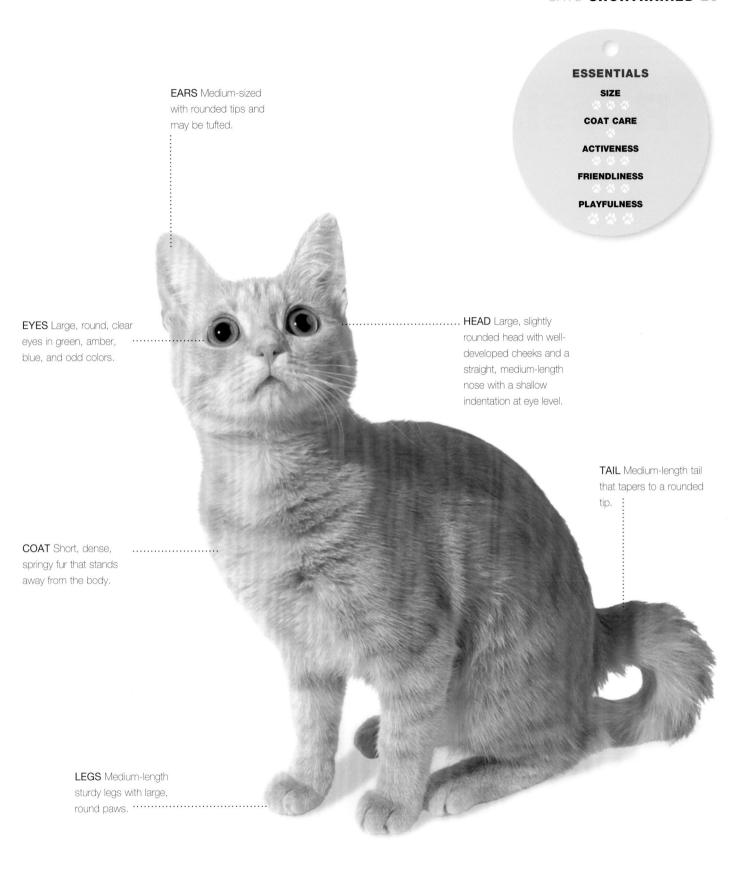

**ESSENTIALS**

SIZE

COAT CARE

ACTIVENESS

FRIENDLINESS

PLAYFULNESS

**EARS** Medium-sized with rounded tips and may be tufted.

**EYES** Large, round, clear eyes in green, amber, blue, and odd colors.

**HEAD** Large, slightly rounded head with well-developed cheeks and a straight, medium-length nose with a shallow indentation at eye level.

**TAIL** Medium-length tail that tapers to a rounded tip.

**COAT** Short, dense, springy fur that stands away from the body.

**LEGS** Medium-length sturdy legs with large, round paws.

# Russian Blue

## RUSSIAN BLUE FACTS

**PHYSIQUE** A medium-sized cat with a long, graceful body. It has a fine-boned frame, good musculature, and long, slender legs.

**COAT** The Russian Blue is, as its name suggests, blue with a silvery sheen. There are also Russian White and Russian Black varieties, which are accepted by some authorities outside the United States.

**TEMPERAMENT** This quiet, shy, and undemanding cat is affectionate, generally good with children, and can make a devoted pet.

**GROOMING** Regular brushing is recommended to keep the Russian Blue's coat looking good.

The origins of the Russian Blue are obscure, but it seems to be native to Russia's cold north. This cat has long been known in that country—Tsar Nicholas II is said to have owned a Russian Blue named Vashka. The breed was probably brought to Britain from the port of Archangelsk, hence its original English name: the Archangel Cat.

The Russian Blue has, over the years, been known by a confusing variety of names—most of them misleading. Among them are Russian Shorthair, Foreign Blue, American Blue, Spanish Blue, Maltese Blue (although the cat has nothing to do with America, Spain, or Malta), or simply The Russian Cat. However, Russian Blue has been the accepted name since the middle years of the 20th century. And rightly so, since this cat almost certainly hails from Russia, and its remarkable blue coat is its outstanding feature.

The coat of the Russian Blue is exceptionally plush—it is often compared to beaver or seal fur. The undercoat is dense and water-resistant while the outer coat consists of remarkably strong "guard" hairs. Some of these top hairs have a transparent tip, which lends the coat a silvery sheen, like polished pewter.

The Russian Blue was well-known in Britain by Victorian times, but, like many breeds, came close to extinction in the course of the Second World War. The breed was revived in the postwar years, partly through the introduction of Siamese blood. This resulted in a more angular Russian Blue than the original, but in Europe at least, the stockier, cobbier norm has been re-established.

The Russian Blue is recognized by most registries only in its original color—but this has not discouraged breeders from trying to create variations on the theme. The Russian White and Russian Black were first bred in New Zealand and have gained some acceptance in the UK. There is also a longhaired version known as the Nebelung—a sword that seems to be a conflation of the Nibelung royal dynasty of Germanic myth, and the German word *Nebel,* meaning "fog."

**EARS** Very large, pointed ears that are placed far apart and set vertically on the head. The insides of the ears are translucent.

**EYES** Wide-set, oval-shaped eyes of brilliant green.

**HEAD** Broad, wedge-shaped head with a medium-length nose, prominent whisker pads, and a blunt muzzle. The neck is long and slender, but can appear shorter due to its thick fur. The nose leather is slate-gray in the United States, blue in the UK.

**COAT** Plush double coat that stands away from the body. The texture is soft and silky.

**LEGS** Slender, elegant legs with small, rounded or oval paws. Pads are pink or mauve in the United States, blue in the UK.

**ESSENTIALS**

**SIZE**

**COAT CARE**

**ACTIVENESS**

**FRIENDLINESS**

**PLAYFULNESS**

**COLOR** Blue-gray with silver-tipped guard hairs, giving the cat a silvery sheen. The color should be even, with no tabby markings.

**TAIL** Long, slightly tapered tail.

# Exotic

## EXOTIC FACTS

🐾 **PHYSIQUE** A compact cat with broad shoulders and chest, short legs, and flattened face.

🐾 **COAT** The Exotic comes in all solid and tortie colors, as well as bicolors. There are also shaded, smoke, tipped, colorpointed, and tabby varieties.

🐾 **TEMPERAMENT** A friendly and companiable cat. The adults are as playful as the kittens, and male cats are often more affectionate than the female.

🐾 **GROOMING** The thick coat needs daily brushing. The coat does not tangle or become matted, like that of the Persian.

At first glance, the Exotic is a paradoxical creature: a shorthaired longhair. It was bred from the Persian, which it closely resembles in every respect, apart from its coat. If anything, its shorter fur enhances its sweet, almost cartoonlike facial features. Its quiet and affectionate nature makes it an ideal lapcat.

The Exotic is an accidental cat, an object lesson in the unpredictable nature of controlled breeding. In the United States in the 1960s, breeders of American Shorthairs crossed their cats with Persians, hoping to produce a shorthair that had the Persian's luminous eyes and lustrous coat. Instead they got the reverse combination: a shorthaired cat with the typically compact body and the teddy-bear face of a Persian.

As it happened, this was a winning combination, since many owners wanted the Persian look without the endless chore of grooming its long coat. The Exotic fulfilled this need, and so is sometimes jokingly referred to as an "easy-care Persian." In the United Kingdom, where Persians are known collectively as Longhairs, the Exotic is generally referred to as the Exotic Shorthair. This name has been adopted in order to underline the fact that the Exotic is a distinctly different breed from its long-haired Persian ancestors.

But as it happens, the Exotic's coat is not all that short. It is certainly longer than the coat of all other shorthairs, although it is not long enough to flow. As regards its other physical traits, the Exotic has all the sentimental appeal of its longhaired antecedents—right down to the irresistible big round eyes and the plaintive voice.

Unfortunately, the Exotic also shares many of the Persian's health problems. The shortened face with its snub nose makes the Exotic prone to respiratory illness. Tear duct problems are also common, because the high snub nose impairs the easy draining of tears down the nasolacrimal duct. Polycystic disease is present in the breed, and its cobby build makes it prone to become overweight unless its diet is carefully managed.

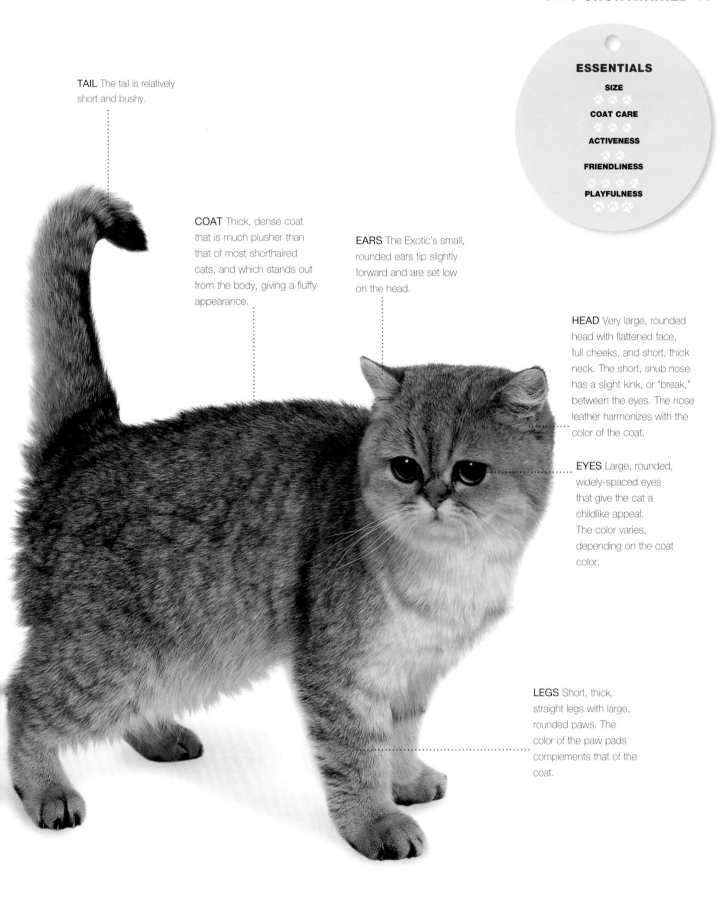

**TAIL** The tail is relatively short and bushy.

**COAT** Thick, dense coat that is much plusher than that of most shorthaired cats, and which stands out from the body, giving a fluffy appearance.

**EARS** The Exotic's small, rounded ears tip slightly forward and are set low on the head.

**HEAD** Very large, rounded head with flattened face, full cheeks, and short, thick neck. The short, snub nose has a slight kink, or "break," between the eyes. The nose leather harmonizes with the color of the coat.

**EYES** Large, rounded, widely-spaced eyes that give the cat a childlike appeal. The color varies, depending on the coat color.

**LEGS** Short, thick, straight legs with large, rounded paws. The color of the paw pads complements that of the coat.

**ESSENTIALS**

**SIZE**

**COAT CARE**

**ACTIVENESS**

**FRIENDLINESS**

**PLAYFULNESS**

# Tonkinese

## TONKINESE FACTS

**PHYSIQUE** A medium-sized, heavy cat that is more slender than the cobby Burmese, but larger and more compact than the svelte Siamese.

**COAT** All solid and tortie colors as well as tabby patterns are accepted in the UK. The United States recognizes natural, champagne, blue, and platinum colors.

**TEMPERAMENT** Most Tonkinese are sociable, affectionate, and have a good sense of play.

**GROOMING** Brush or wipe with a silk cloth regularly to keep the coat in good condition.

The Tonkinese is the North American product of two much-loved cats: the Siamese and the Burmese. Its status as a separate breed is sometimes disputed—because a litter of four is likely to produce two Tonkinese, one Siamese, and one Burmese. But fans of the Tonk insist that it is a genuine breed that displays all the best characteristics of both its ancestors.

The first Siamese-Burmese crosses were the result of spontaneous interbreeding. The "Chocolate Siamese," which was imported into England in the 19th century, may have been such an accidental mating. In the 1930s, another crossbreed, a walnut-colored female called Wong Mau, was imported into the United States and used to found the Burmese breed.

It was not until the 1950s that a systematic breeding program to recreate the Burmese-Siamese cross began. The resulting cat was then dubbed a "Golden Siamese," but it did not gain recognition at that time. It was first recognized by registries in Canada in the 1960s, then quickly won acceptance in the United States and in Europe.

While arguments persist among experts as to whether the Tonkinese should be considered a breed, there is no doubt about this cat's widespread appeal among cat lovers in general. The Tonk is prized for its unique "mink" coat pattern, which has darker points merging almost imperceptibly into a lighter-toned body. The popularity of the Tonk is also due to the fact that it is known to be almost doggishly friendly: it has an acrobatic liveliness; it will fetch toys when you throw them, it will show a warm-hearted interest in anyone who comes to the door. In a word, it is as extrovert and gregarious as its Siamese ancestor, but without the Siamese's voluble miaow.

The playful nature of the Tonkinese means that owners should take care to make their environment safe. "Tonks," as they are known, are indoor cats, so doors and screens should be secured. Their need for company means that many owners find that two Tonks are less trouble than one, as they will happily amuse each other.

**HEAD** The head shape is a wedge with a blunt muzzle and high cheekbones.

**EARS** Medium-sized ears that are broad at the head and narrow to an oval tip.

**EYES** Widely set, almond-shaped eyes. The color should be bluish-green.

**COAT** Close-lying, medium-short coat that has a fine texture and a natural luster.

**COLOR** The body color fades to a lighter shade on the underbelly and blends into the darker points (mask, ears, feet, and tail).

**ESSENTIALS**

SIZE

COAT CARE

ACTIVENESS

FRIENDLINESS

PLAYFULNESS

**NOSE** The color of the nose pad should correspond to the color of the coat.

**PAWS** Oval paws with pads that complement the coat coloring.

**LEGS** Slim, well-muscled legs. The back legs are slightly longer than the front ones.

# Singapura

## SINGAPURA FACTS

**PHYSIQUE** The Singapura is one of the smaller pedigree breeds. It has a compact, medium-length body and legs that are well-muscled but elegant.

**COAT** The distinctive coloring is known as "sepia agouti." It is warm ivory on the body with dark (sepia) brown ticking.

**TEMPERAMENT** A gentle, reserved cat with a sweet nature. The Singapura likes company and can be extremely affectionate.

**GROOMING** Brush regularly, or wipe with a silk cloth, to keep the coat in good condition.

This beautiful cat was once culled by the authorities in its native Singapore, and dubbed the "drain cat" after the place where it took refuge. Today it is used as a mascot by the Singapore Tourist Board, which has given it a new name that fits its affectionate nature—"Kucinta," or the "love cat."

In 1975, breeders Hal and Tommy Meadows brought three cats—Pusse, Ticle and Tes—into the United States from Singapore. They used these distinctive-looking cats as the founding stock for a breeding program. The cats' popularity grew, and within seven years the Singapura—named after the Malayan word for Singapore—was recognized in North America as a natural breed. All registered Singapuras today originate from the Meadows' breeding program. However, the cats are still relatively rare.

There has been some controversy about the origins of the Singapura. Although there are undoubtedly feral cats living in Singapore that resemble the pedigree cat, some people have speculated that Burmese and Abyssinian cats were used to help create the pedigree breed. One piece of supporting evidence is the fact that the Singapura tends to be larger than its street equivalent, which could suggest that new breeding stock has been introduced. However, its greater size could also be due to the better diet it receives as a domestic animal.

Whether the Singapura is a natural breed or not, it is undoubtedly an unusually beautiful creature. Its delicate appearance belies its muscular stature—the Singapura is surprisingly heavy when you pick it up. Its eyes and ears are large in relation to its head, which makes it look alert and lively.

Unlike most of the other Oriental cats, the Singapura is naturally quiet and undemanding. It is generally reserved but once it has learned to trust its owner, the Singapura can be remarkably responsive. It can also be very playful in the right environment. Despite its street ancestry, it enjoys a quiet indoor life.

**HEAD** Rounded head with a short, blunt muzzle and a blunt nose, with a salmon-colored leather outlined in black.

**EARS** Large ears that are wide at the base and deeply cupped, with a rounded point.

**EYES** Very large, almond-shaped eyes with a slight slant. They are brilliant yellow, green, or hazel in color, with an attractive black outline.

**COAT** Short, close-lying coat that has a fine, silky texture.

**ESSENTIALS**

SIZE

COAT CARE

ACTIVENESS

FRIENDLINESS

PLAYFULNESS

**COLOR** Markings on the back of the legs but not on the front. The underparts of the body are pale. There should be at least two bands of dark banding interspersed with light on each hair, starting light next to the body and ending in a dark tip.

**LEGS** Strong legs that are muscular at the top and taper to small, oval paws with brown pads.

**TAIL** Blunt-tipped, slender tail, slightly shorter than the length of the body.

# Seal Point Siamese

## SEAL POINT SIAMESE FACTS

**PHYSIQUE** The Siamese is the archetypal Oriental cat: sleek, lithe, and elegant with fine bone structure and good muscle tone.

**COAT** The Seal Point is one of four classic colors accepted in the Siamese. Cats with other point colors are Colorpoint Shorthairs in the United States, but Siamese elsewhere.

**TEMPERAMENT** The Seal Point Siamese is naturally extrovert and affectionate. It is extremely chatty and can be demanding.

**GROOMING** Brush regularly, and stroke with a silk cloth to bring out the sheen of the coat.

The origins of the Seal Point Siamese are as dark and unknowable as its inscrutable face. One theory says that the breed is a mutation that came about in Siam (present-day Thailand) 500 years ago. Another says that the first Siamese were carried to Siam by Egyptian traders. Whatever their history, there is no doubting their regal demeanour.

The Siamese cat is surely the most recognizable of all breeds. And yet there is considerable disagreement as to how it should look. Some aficionados, primarily in the United States, favor a slim, almost emaciated build—and breed with a view to enhancing those traits. Others maintain that a true Siamese is far stockier than present taste dictates, and that its head should be "apple-shaped" rather than markedly triangular.

The first Siamese to make their way to the West were Seal Points, and they resembled the apple-headed ideal more than they did the svelte and angular variant that we now know. The first Siamese (one was exhibited in London in 1871) were also afflicted with a marked squint and a kink in the tail. Such peculiarities were at first encouraged as distinctive Siamese traits, but breeders soon decided that it was better to eliminate them. The key defining feature of the Seal Point Siamese, and indeed of all Siamese, is the coat pattern, which always consists of a pale body with darker extremities. This pattern comes about because the Siamese has a gene that inhibits pigmentation in parts of the body where the temperature is high. If the torso of the Siamese were cooler, its body fur would darken—which does in fact occur in old age. Conversely, if any of the extremities become warm—say, if a foot is bandaged after an injury—then the dark pigmentation temporarily disappears. Temperamentally, the Siamese is a thing apart. This cat can be aloof, demanding, one might almost say aristocratic. But at the same time it is extremely gregarious and craves attention. It is also by far the most vocal of cats, with a large repertoire of yowls, mews, and squeals.

**ESSENTIALS**

SIZE

COAT CARE

ACTIVENESS

FRIENDLINESS

PLAYFULNESS

**COLOR** The body is fawn to cream, and lighter on the belly and chest. It contrasts with the dark-brown coloring on the mask, ears, legs, and tail.

**EARS** Huge ears that are wide at the base and pointed at the tips, forming a triangle with the head.

**HEAD** An elongated wedge-shaped head that tapers into the well-defined muzzle and is carried on a slender, elegant neck. The nose is long and perfectly straight in profile, with dark-brown nose leather.

**EYES** Slanted, almond-shaped, medium-sized eyes in deep, clear blue.

**COAT** Close-lying, medium-short coat that has a fine texture and a natural luster.

**TAIL** The tail is long and narrows to a slender point.

**LEGS** Long, slender legs that taper into the paws. The hind legs are longer than the forelegs.

**PAWS** Small, oval-shaped paws with dark-brown pads.

# Blue Point Siamese

## BLUE POINT SIAMESE FACTS

**PHYSIQUE** The Siamese is the archetypal Oriental cat: sleek, lithe, and elegant with fine bone structure and good muscle tone.

**COAT** The Blue Point is one of four classic colors accepted in the Siamese. Cats with other point colors are classed as Colorpoint Shorthairs in the United States, but are classified as Siamese elsewhere.

**TEMPERAMENT** The Siamese Blue Point is naturally extrovert and affectionate. It is extremely chatty and can be demanding.

**GROOMING** Brush regularly, and stroke with a silk cloth to bring out the sheen of the coat.

The Blue Point is one of the four classic colors for a Siamese cat. It has been a known Siamese variant for well over a hundred years. It is possible that the dilute "blue gene" is ultimately derived from Thailand's second most famous cat, the blue-coated Korat.

**HEAD** An elongated wedge-shaped head that tapers into the well-defined muzzle and is carried on a slender, elegant neck. The nose is long and perfectly straight in profile, with slate-colored or blue nose leather.

**EYES** Slanted, almond-shaped, medium-sized eyes in deep, clear blue.

**EARS** Huge ears that are wide at the base and pointed at the tips, forming a triangle with the head.

**COAT** The coat is close-lying, short, and fine, with a natural sheen.

**COLOR** The body is cold bluish-white, shading to white on the stomach and chest. The points are blue-gray.

**TAIL** The tail is long and narrows to a slender point.

**LEGS** Long, slender legs that taper into the paws. The hind legs are longer than the forelegs.

**PAWS** Small, oval-shaped paws with slate-colored or blue pads.

## ESSENTIALS

SIZE

COAT CARE

ACTIVENESS

FRIENDLINESS

PLAYFULNESS

# Chocolate Point Siamese

There is some natural variation in Siamese coloring, and this genetic fact has been exploited by breeders to produce the Chocolate Point. This variant is the product of crosses between lighter-hued cats. Its coat is ivory where the naturally occurring color is closer to fawn, and its pointing is "milk chocolate" rather than dark brown.

## CHOCOLATE POINT SIAMESE FACTS

**PHYSIQUE** This is the archetypal Oriental cat: sleek, lithe, and elegant, with fine bone structure and good muscle tone.

**COAT** The Chocolate Point is one of four classic colors accepted in the Siamese. Cats with other point colors are classed as Colorpoint Shorthairs in the United States, but Siamese elsewhere.

**TEMPERAMENT** The Siamese Chocolate Point is naturally extrovert and affectionate. It is extremely chatty and can be demanding.

**GROOMING** Brush regularly, and stroke with a silk cloth to bring out the sheen of the coat.

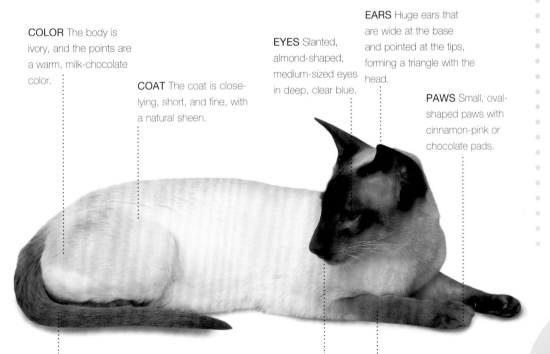

**COLOR** The body is ivory, and the points are a warm, milk-chocolate color.

**COAT** The coat is close-lying, short, and fine, with a natural sheen.

**EYES** Slanted, almond-shaped, medium-sized eyes in deep, clear blue.

**EARS** Huge ears that are wide at the base and pointed at the tips, forming a triangle with the head.

**PAWS** Small, oval-shaped paws with cinnamon-pink or chocolate pads.

**TAIL** The tail is long and narrows to a slender point.

**HEAD** An elongated, wedge-shaped head that tapers into the well-defined muzzle and is carried on a slender neck. The nose is long and perfectly straight in profile, with cinnamon-pink or chocolate nose leather.

**LEGS** Long, slender legs that taper into the paws. The hind legs are longer than the forelegs.

## ESSENTIALS

**SIZE**

**COAT CARE**

**ACTIVENESS**

**FRIENDLINESS**

**PLAYFULNESS**

# Lilac Point Siamese

## LILAC POINT SIAMESE FACTS

**PHYSIQUE** This Siamese is the archetypal Oriental cat: sleek, lithe, and elegant with fine bone structure and good muscle tone.

**COAT** The Lilac Point is one of four colors accepted in the Siamese. Cats with other point colors are classed as Colorpoint Shorthairs in the United States, but Siamese elsewhere.

**TEMPERAMENT** The Siamese Lilac Point is naturally extrovert and affectionate. It is extremely chatty and can be demanding.

**GROOMING** Brush regularly, and stroke with a silk cloth to bring out the sheen of the coat.

**ESSENTIALS**

SIZE

COAT CARE

ACTIVENESS

FRIENDLINESS

PLAYFULNESS

The Lilac Point Siamese is an even more dilute form of the Chocolate Point. In the United States it is sometimes known as the "Frost," because the icy color of its body is very close to snow-white. The pointing is blue-gray with a subtle hint of lavender that perfectly matches its pink nose and paw pads.

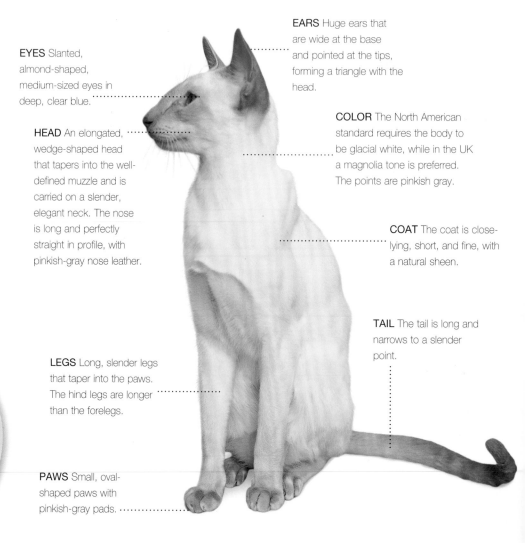

**EYES** Slanted, almond-shaped, medium-sized eyes in deep, clear blue.

**EARS** Huge ears that are wide at the base and pointed at the tips, forming a triangle with the head.

**HEAD** An elongated, wedge-shaped head that tapers into the well-defined muzzle and is carried on a slender, elegant neck. The nose is long and perfectly straight in profile, with pinkish-gray nose leather.

**COLOR** The North American standard requires the body to be glacial white, while in the UK a magnolia tone is preferred. The points are pinkish gray.

**COAT** The coat is close-lying, short, and fine, with a natural sheen.

**TAIL** The tail is long and narrows to a slender point.

**LEGS** Long, slender legs that taper into the paws. The hind legs are longer than the forelegs.

**PAWS** Small, oval-shaped paws with pinkish-gray pads.

# Red Point Colorpoint Shorthair

The Red Point is one of the newer Siamese color variations. This and other varieties outside the four "classic" colors are termed Colorpoint Shorthairs n the United States, but accepted as Siamese elsewhere. Whatever its appellation, the Red Point is a beautiful cat with blue eyes that make a striking contrast with its apricot pointing.

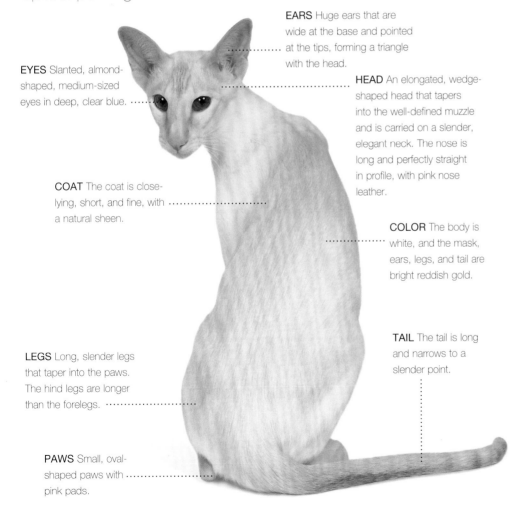

**EARS** Huge ears that are wide at the base and pointed at the tips, forming a triangle with the head.

**EYES** Slanted, almond-shaped, medium-sized eyes in deep, clear blue.

**HEAD** An elongated, wedge-shaped head that tapers into the well-defined muzzle and is carried on a slender, elegant neck. The nose is long and perfectly straight in profile, with pink nose leather.

**COAT** The coat is close-lying, short, and fine, with a natural sheen.

**COLOR** The body is white, and the mask, ears, legs, and tail are bright reddish gold.

**TAIL** The tail is long and narrows to a slender point.

**LEGS** Long, slender legs that taper into the paws. The hind legs are longer than the forelegs.

**PAWS** Small, oval-shaped paws with pink pads.

## RED POINT COLORPOINT SHORTHAIR FACTS

**PHYSIQUE** This is the archetypal Oriental cat: sleek, lithe, and elegant, with fine bone structure and good muscle tone.

**COAT** The Chocolate Point is one of four classic colors accepted in the Siamese. Cats with other point colors are classed as Colorpoint Shorthairs in the United States, but Siamese elsewhere.

**TEMPERAMENT** The Siamese Chocolate Point is naturally extrovert and affectionate. It is extremely chatty and can be demanding.

**GROOMING** Brush regularly, and stroke with a silk cloth to bring out the sheen of the coat.

**ESSENTIALS**

**SIZE**

**COAT CARE**

**ACTIVENESS**

**FRIENDLINESS**

**PLAYFULNESS**

# Cream Point Colorpoint Shorthair

## CREAM POINT COLORPOINT SHORTHAIR FACTS

**PHYSIQUE** A medium-sized, lithe, and slender cat, with fine bone structure and good muscle tone.

**COAT** Cream is one of two solid point colors accepted in the United States. Elsewhere, fawn, caramel, apricot, and cinnamon colors are recognized, and the cats are classed as Siamese.

**TEMPERAMENT** This cat is naturally extrovert and affectionate. As with other Colorpoint Shorthairs, it is chatty and can be demanding.

**GROOMING** Brush regularly, and rub with a silk cloth to bring out the sheen of the coat.

The Cream Point Siamese is a dilute form of the Red Point. The red gene was introduced to the Siamese line in the 1930s through crosses to Red Tabby Longhairs, but then practically died out. The cats were bred anew in the 1940s, and became generally accepted as a distinct breed in the 1960s.

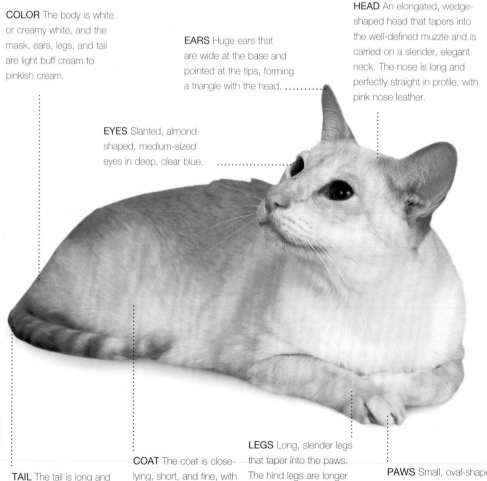

**COLOR** The body is white or creamy white, and the mask, ears, legs, and tail are light buff cream to pinkish cream.

**EARS** Huge ears that are wide at the base and pointed at the tips, forming a triangle with the head.

**HEAD** An elongated, wedge-shaped head that tapers into the well-defined muzzle and is carried on a slender, elegant neck. The nose is long and perfectly straight in profile, with pink nose leather.

**EYES** Slanted, almond-shaped, medium-sized eyes in deep, clear blue.

**TAIL** The tail is long and narrows to a slender point.

**COAT** The coat is close-lying, short, and fine, with a natural sheen.

**LEGS** Long, slender legs that taper into the paws. The hind legs are longer than the forelegs.

**PAWS** Small, oval-shaped paws with pink pads.

## ESSENTIALS

**SIZE**

**COAT CARE**

**ACTIVENESS**

**FRIENDLINESS**

**PLAYFULNESS**

# Tortie Point
# Colorpoint Shorthair

Tortie Points, like Red Points, are the natural consequence of introducing the red gene into the Siamese line. They come in the traditional four colors as well as in newer ones such as cinnamon. The red and cream mottled effect on the pointing should be overlaid on the base color in a random pattern.

## TORTIE POINT COLORPOINT SHORTHAIR FACTS

**PHYSIQUE** A medium-sized, lithe, and slender cat, with fine bone structure and good muscle tone.

**COAT** Seal, chocolate, blue-cream, and lilac-cream are the most widely recognized main colors. Outside the United States, other colors, including cinnamon, caramel, and fawn, are also accepted.

**TEMPERAMENT** This cat is naturally extrovert and affectionate. It is chatty and can be demanding.

**GROOMING** Brush regularly, and rub with a silk cloth to bring out the sheen of the coat.

**HEAD** The wedge-shaped head tapers into a well-defined muzzle, with a slender, elegant neck and long, straight nose—nose leather complements the main color of the points.

**EYES** Slanted, almond-shaped, medium-sized eyes in deep, clear blue.

**COLOR** The body is pale, forming a distinct contrast to the darker points, which are mottled with red, cream, or both.

**EARS** Huge ears that are wide at the base and pointed at the tips, forming a triangle with the head.

**TAIL** The tail is long and narrows to a slender point.

**COAT** The coat is close-lying, short, and fine, with a natural sheen.

**LEGS** Long, slender legs that taper into the paws. The hind legs are longer than the forelegs.

**PAWS** Small, oval-shaped paws with pads that harmonize with the main color of the points.

## ESSENTIALS

**SIZE**

**COAT CARE**

**ACTIVENESS**

**FRIENDLINESS**

**PLAYFULNESS**

# Lynx Point Colorpoint Shorthair

## LYNX POINT COLORPOINT SHORTHAIR FACTS

**PHYSIQUE** A medium-sized, lithe, and slender cat, with fine bone structure and good muscle tone.

**COAT** The Lynx (Tabby) Point comes in all the recognized solid and tortie colors.

**TEMPERAMENT** This cat is naturally extrovert and affectionate. It is chatty and can be demanding.

**GROOMING** Brush regularly, and rub with a silk cloth to bring out the sheen of the coat.

The Lynx Point is known as the Tabby Point outside the United States and the cat is classed as a Siamese. The tabby markings on the points contrast beautifully with the pale body, although some ghost striping or ticking may be seen here. Originally, this variation was recognized only in the seal, blue, chocolate, and lilac, but variants now include all the tortie colors.

**COLOR** The body is pale, forming a distinct contrast with the colorful points. Tabby markings include a "thumbprint" pale patch on the marked ears, an "M" on the forehead, stripes on the face and legs, and rings on the tail.

**EARS** Huge ears that are wide at the base and pointed at the tips, forming a triangle with the head.

**EYES** Slanted, almond-shaped, medium-sized eyes in deep, clear blue.

**HEAD** An elongated, wedge-shaped head that tapers into the well-defined muzzle and is carried on a slender, elegant neck. The nose is long and perfectly straight in profile, with nose leather that harmonizes with the main color of the points.

**TAIL** The tail is long and narrows to a slender point.

**COAT** The coat is close-lying, short, and fine, with a natural sheen.

**LEGS** Long, slender legs that taper into the paws. The hind legs are longer than the forelegs.

**PAWS** Small, oval-shaped paws with pads that harmonize with the main color of the points.

## ESSENTIALS

**SIZE**

**COAT CARE**

**ACTIVENESS**

**FRIENDLINESS**

**PLAYFULNESS**

# Blue Oriental Shorthair

The Oriental Shorthair is a Siamese cat that lacks the characteristic Siamese pointing. Instead it has a coat with an alover pattern or color, such as this striking Blue Oriental Shorthair. In the United States, longhaired and shorthaired Orientals are classed together as the same breed. Elsewhere, they are seen as separate breeds: the Oriental Shorthair, and the Oriental Longhair.

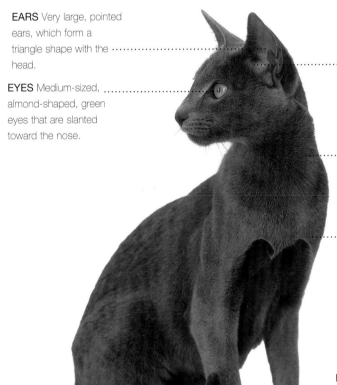

**EARS** Very large, pointed ears, which form a triangle shape with the head.

**EYES** Medium-sized, almond-shaped, green eyes that are slanted toward the nose.

**HEAD** Elongated, wedge-shaped head carried on a long, elegant neck. The nose is long and straight with blue leather, and the tapering muzzle is well-defined.

**COAT** Short, fine-textured, close-lying coat with a glossy or satiny finish.

**COLOR** The color ranges from pale blue to slate-gray. The color should be even from the tips to the roots of the hairs, and all over the body.

**LEGS** Long, slender legs that taper into small, oval-shaped paws with blue pads. The hind legs are longer than the forelegs.

**TAIL** Long, elegant tail that narrows into a fine point.

## BLUE ORIENTAL SHORTHAIR FACTS

**PHYSIQUE** A classic Oriental cat, with a long, lithe body and good muscle tone.

**COAT** Blue is one of various recognized solid colors that also include white, black, and the more unusual fawn and cinnamon. There are also Smoke, Shaded, Tortoiseshell, Bicolor, and Tabby Oriental Shorthairs.

**TEMPERAMENT** A very sociable cat that is highly inquisitive and playful. Like the Siamese, it is chatty and demanding.

**GROOMING** Regular brushing and stroking with a gloved hand helps to keep the coat shiny.

### ESSENTIALS

SIZE

COAT CARE

ACTIVENESS

FRIENDLINESS

PLAYFULNESS

# Cream Oriental Shorthair

## CREAM ORIENTAL SHORTHAIR FACTS

**PHYSIQUE** A classic Oriental cat, with a long, lithe body and good muscle tone.

**COAT** Cream is one of various recognized solid colors that include white, black, fawn, and cinnamon. Smoke, Shaded, Tortoiseshell, Bicolor, and Tabby Oriental Shorthairs are also recognized.

**TEMPERAMENT** A very sociable cat that is highly inquisitive and playful. Like the Siamese, the Oriental Shorthair is chatty and demanding.

**GROOMING** Regular brushing and stroking with a gloved hand helps to keep the coat shiny.

The Cream Oriental Shorthair is one of many Siamese-type cats with a one-color rather than pointed coat. The self, or solid, colors used to be known as Foreign Shorthairs outside the United States, but now only the white variant retains the name Foreign White. That cat is the only Oriental to have the blue eyes of the Siamese; other Orientals have eyes of clear, brilliant green.

**COLOR** The cream color should be even from the tips to the roots of the hairs, and all over the body.

**EARS** Very large, pointed ears, which form a triangle shape with the head.

**EYES** Medium-sized, almond-shaped eyes that are slanted toward the nose. Green is desirable but colors may vary.

**TAIL** Long, elegant tail that narrows into a fine point.

**HEAD** Elongated, wedge-shaped head carried on a long, elegant neck. The nose is long and straight with pink leather, and the tapering muzzle is well-defined.

**LEGS** Long, slender legs that taper into small, oval-shaped paws with pink pads. The hind legs are longer than the forelegs.

**COAT** Short, fine-textured, close-lying coat with a glossy or satiny finish.

## ESSENTIALS

SIZE

COAT CARE

ACTIVENESS

FRIENDLINESS

PLAYFULNESS

# Chestnut Brown Oriental Shorthair

The Chestnut Brown is, in effect, a Chocolate Oriental Shorthair. It is known as a Havana in the UK because its color resembles that of a Cuban cigar. It is not to be confused with the cat known in the United States as a Havana Brown, which is a chocolate-colored cat with a body shape akin to a Russian Blue.

## CHESTNUT BROWN ORIENTAL SHORTHAIR FACTS

**PHYSIQUE** This is a classic Oriental cat, with a long, lithe body and good muscle tone.

**COAT** Chestnut (brown) is one of various recognized solid colors that also include white, black, and the more unusual fawn and cinnamon. Smoke, Shaded, Tortoise-shell, Bicolor and Tabby Oriental Shorthairs are also recognized.

**TEMPERAMENT** A very sociable cat that is highly inquisitive and playful. Like the Siamese, it is chatty and demanding.

**GROOMING** Regular brushing and stroking with a gloved hand helps to keep the coat shiny.

**HEAD** Elongated, wedge-shaped head carried on a long, elegant neck. The nose is long and straight with chestnut or pinkish brown leather, and the tapering muzzle is well-defined.

**EARS** Very large, pointed ears, which form a triangle shape with the head.

**EYES** Medium-sized, almond-shaped eyes that are slanted toward the nose. Green is desirable but colors may vary.

**COLOR** Rich chestnut. The color should be even from the tips to the roots of the hairs, and all over the body.

**COAT** Short, fine-textured, close-lying coat with a glossy or satiny finish.

**TAIL** Long, elegant tail that narrows into a fine point.

**LEGS** Long, slender legs that taper into small, oval-shaped paws with cinnamon or pinkish-brown pads. The hind legs are longer than the forelegs.

**ESSENTIALS**

SIZE

COAT CARE

ACTIVENESS

FRIENDLINESS

PLAYFULNESS

# Shaded Oriental Shorthair

## SHADED ORIENTAL SHORTHAIR FACTS

**PHYSIQUE** A classic Oriental cat, with a long, lithe body and good muscle tone.

**COAT** Shaded cats come in all the recognized Oriental colors. The United States accepts only silver colors, while both standard and silver colors are recognized in the UK.

**TEMPERAMENT** A very sociable cat that is highly inquisitive and playful. Like the Siamese, it is chatty and demanding.

**GROOMING** Regular brushing and stroking with a gloved hand helps to keep the coat shiny.

Shaded Orientals have a pale coat that is tipped with color. The tipping can be restricted to the ends of the hairs or reach a depth of halfway down—and the overall effect is of a colored mantle. In the Smoke Orientals, the tipping is much deeper so that the cat can appear to be solid colored, until it moves and exposes its pale undercoat.

**EARS** Very large, pointed ears, which form a triangle shape with the head.

**EYES** Medium-sized, almond-shaped eyes that are slanted toward the nose. The color is vivid green.

**COLOR** The undercoat is white in the silver colors (pale in the Standard colors), with tipping on the face, sides, and tail. The chin and undersides are white (or pale).

**COAT** Short, fine-textured, close-lying coat with a glossy or satiny finish.

**HEAD** Elongated, wedge-shaped head carried on a long elegant neck. The nose is long and straight and the tapering muzzle is well-defined. The nose leather harmonizes with the color of the tipping.

**LEGS** Long, slender legs that taper into small, oval-shaped paws with pads that harmonize with the color of the tipping. The hind legs are longer than the forelegs.

**TAIL** Long elegant tail that narrows into a fine point.

## ESSENTIALS

**SIZE**

**COAT CARE**

**ACTIVENESS**

**FRIENDLINESS**

**PLAYFULNESS**

# Bicolor Oriental Shorthair

Bicolor Orientals have been recognized since 1995 in North America. These cats have pure white undersides, legs, and chest, and a distinctive inverted "V" blaze on the face. All the established colors and patterns are allowed. Bicolors are recognized by other international registries, but they are only just starting to gain acceptance in the UK.

## BICOLOR ORIENTAL SHORTHAIR FACTS

**PHYSIQUE** This is a classic Oriental cat, with a long, lithe body and good muscle tone.

**COAT** White with patches of any accepted solid, shaded, smoke, or tortoiseshell color or tabby pattern. There are pointed and van-pointed varieties as well as the standard bicolor.

**TEMPERAMENT** A very sociable cat that is highly inquisitive and playful. Like the Siamese, it is chatty and demanding.

**GROOMING** Regular brushing and stroking with a gloved hand helps to keep the coat shiny.

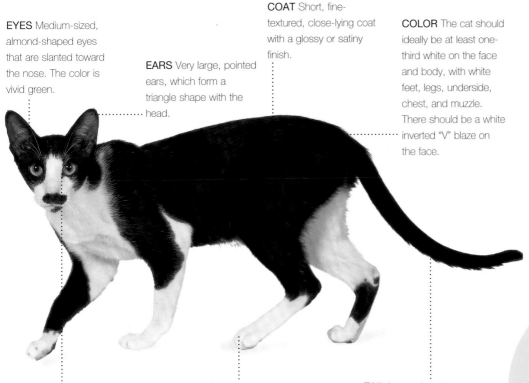

**EYES** Medium-sized, almond-shaped eyes that are slanted toward the nose. The color is vivid green.

**EARS** Very large, pointed ears, which form a triangle shape with the head.

**COAT** Short, fine-textured, close-lying coat with a glossy or satiny finish.

**COLOR** The cat should ideally be at least one-third white on the face and body, with white feet, legs, underside, chest, and muzzle. There should be a white inverted "V" blaze on the face.

**HEAD** Elongated, wedge-shaped head carried on a long, elegant neck. The nose is long and straight and the tapering muzzle is well-defined. The nose leather harmonizes with the colored part of the coat.

**LEGS** Long, slender legs that taper into small, oval-shaped paws with pads that harmonize with the colored part of the coat. The hind legs are longer than the forelegs.

**TAIL** Long, elegant tail that narrows into a fine point.

## ESSENTIALS

SIZE

COAT CARE

ACTIVENESS

FRIENDLINESS

PLAYFULNESS

# Korat

## KORAT FACTS

**PHYSIQUE** The Korat has a medium-sized, muscular body with a broad chest and well-spaced forelegs.

**COAT** The only recognized color is blue. The coat is lighter at the base and darkens just before the tip, which is silvery. The silvering creates an attractive, aura-like effect.

**TEMPERAMENT** These active and vocal cats are very gentle and easily startled. If treated with care, they are highly affectionate and are good with children.

**GROOMING** The Korat benefits from daily grooming to keep the coat in good condition.

The silvery-gray Korat is one of the most ancient and beautiful of natural breeds. It takes its name from Cao Nguyen Khorat, the province of Thailand from which it hails. In its homeland the Korat is sometimes called the "cloud-colored cat," and it has long been revered there as a symbol of good fortune.

There is a picture of the Korat in a medieval Thai text known as the Cat-Book Poems. Alongside the painted image is a lovely lyric that describes this special cat: "The hairs are smooth, with roots like clouds and tips like silver; the eyes shine like dewdrops on a lotus leaf." In Siam, as Thailand was once known, people associated the Korat's dark fur with the color of storm clouds, and so the cat was often used in the rain-making ceremonies that took place at the end of the dry season. The Korat's green eyes were also symbolically significant: they were thought to resemble the color of young rice, and so stood for prosperity. To symbolize this, a pair of Korats were often given to a bride on her wedding day.

In fact, the Korat was only ever given as a gift—it was never sold. For this reason, it remained unknown in the West until relatively recently. The first Korat was exhibited in London in 1894 by a young man named Mr Spearman. It is not known how he came by it, but he had recently returned from Siam. The breed was not heard of again until 1959, when a pair was presented to the American ambassador to Thailand. They were called Narra and Darra, and they were the foundation pair of an American breeding program. They were recognized as a pedigree breed in the United States in 1966. The Korat came to Britain in 1972. Korat males are believed to make very good fathers if left alone with their litter. Their parental instincts also extend to their human owners:

they are known to be particularly loving and tolerant toward small children.

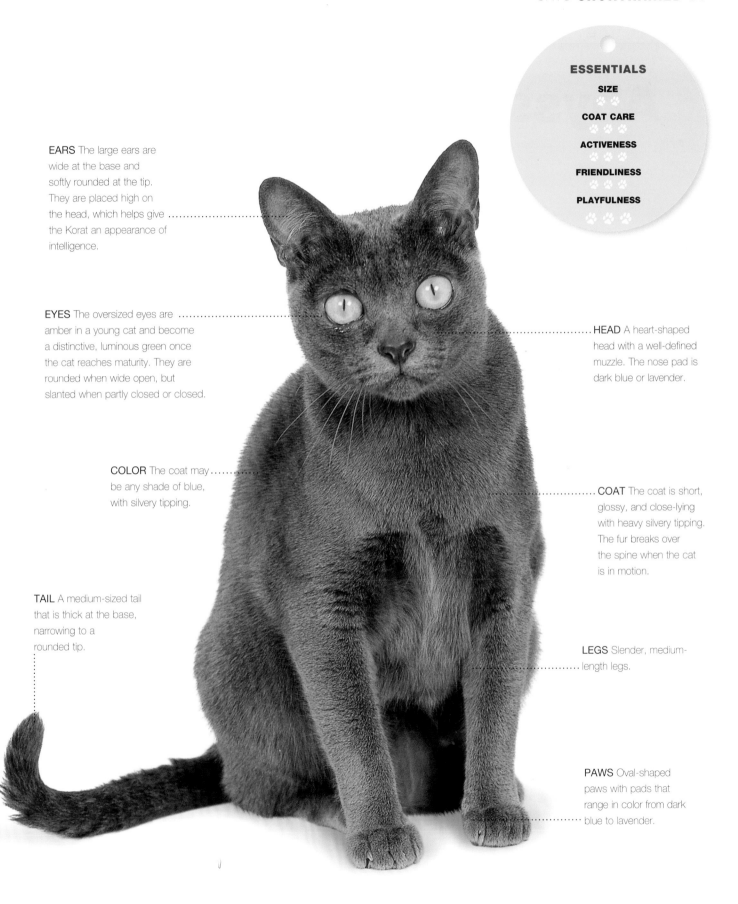

**ESSENTIALS**

SIZE

COAT CARE

ACTIVENESS

FRIENDLINESS

PLAYFULNESS

**EARS** The large ears are wide at the base and softly rounded at the tip. They are placed high on the head, which helps give the Korat an appearance of intelligence.

**EYES** The oversized eyes are amber in a young cat and become a distinctive, luminous green once the cat reaches maturity. They are rounded when wide open, but slanted when partly closed or closed.

**COLOR** The coat may be any shade of blue, with silvery tipping.

**TAIL** A medium-sized tail that is thick at the base, narrowing to a rounded tip.

**HEAD** A heart-shaped head with a well-defined muzzle. The nose pad is dark blue or lavender.

**COAT** The coat is short, glossy, and close-lying with heavy silvery tipping. The fur breaks over the spine when the cat is in motion.

**LEGS** Slender, medium-length legs.

**PAWS** Oval-shaped paws with pads that range in color from dark blue to lavender.

# Abyssinian

## ABYSSINIAN FACTS

🐾 **PHYSIQUE** The Abyssinian has a medium-long, lithe body with an elegantly arched neck.

🐾 **COAT** Ruddy (this is termed "usual" in the UK), red (sorrel), fawn, and blue are the four colors recognized·in the United States. Other authorities accept a wider range of colors, including lilac and chocolate, tortoiseshell colors and silver colors.

🐾 **TEMPERAMENT** A quiet, but highly active cat that loves to play. It is very sociable and needs plenty of attention.

🐾 **GROOMING** Daily brushing will keep the coat in good condition.

Unlike many breeds with geographical names, the Abyssinian genuinely hails from Abyssinia. The ancestors of modern "Abys" were brought to England from the African state of Abyssinia (modern-day Ethiopia) in the middle of the 19th century. This is a freedom-loving and particularly handsome cat with a nature as warm as its ruddy-colored coat.

Abyssinia lies to the south of Egypt, and popular mythology has for a long time equated the Abyssinian with the cats worshipped by the ancient Egyptians. It is certainly the case that the Aby's body shape resembles statuettes of the cat-god Bast and paintings of cats on temple walls in the Nile Delta. There is also something about the cat's bearing when seated—alert, knowing, proud—that puts one in mind of the eternal Sphinx.

But we cannot know for certain if the Abyssinian was known to the pharaohs. So, for all practical purposes, the history of the Abyssinian begins in 1867, when the armed forces of the British Empire waged a brief, one-sided war against the Emperor of Abyssinia. Some of the British soldiers who fought in Abyssinia acquired cats, one of which was a red-coated female called Zula (the name of the Abyssinian port where the British established their base). This cat, along with other specimens, provided the foundation stock for the Abyssinian breed.

Until the end of the nineteenth century, the Abyssinian was often referred to as the "Hare Cat" or "Bunny Cat". These rather undignified names refer to the fact that, like rabbits and hares, it has a "ticked" coat, meaning that each hair has several bands of darker coloring. The ticking is one of the Aby's distinctive features.

The breed almost became extinct in Britain in the first years of the 20th century, but a number of fine specimens were exported to the United States, where it was bred successfully and became popular. The brownish color of the Abyssinian is termed "ruddy" or "usual," although other colors have been developed.

**ESSENTIALS**

SIZE

COAT CARE

ACTIVENESS

FRIENDLINESS

PLAYFULNESS

**EARS** Large, broad ears that are cupped at the head and have rounded tips. Short hairs on the ears should be a darker color than the coat.

**TAIL** A long tail that is thick at the base, narrowing to a rounded tip that is darker in color.

**EYES** Expressive, black-rimmed, almond-shaped eyes in deep gold or green.

**HEAD** A slightly rounded, wedge-shaped head that flows seamlessly into the arched neck. The nose has a slight "break," or kink, and aligns neatly with the chin. The color of the nose pad complements that of the coat.

**COAT** The short, thick, soft coat is ticked evenly, with each hair having alternate bands of light and dark. There is no ticking on the underparts.

**LEGS** The Abyssinian stands tall on long, slender legs, giving the impression of walking on tiptoe.

**PAWS** Small, oval-shaped paws. The paw pads harmonize with the Abyssinian's coat color.

# Sokoke

## SOKOKE FACTS

🐾 **PHYSIQUE** Medium-sized cat with a slim, muscular body, prominent chest, and long, elegant legs.

🐾 **COAT** The Sokoke is a brown tabby with a sandy background color and black to brown markings.

🐾 **TEMPERAMENT** A highly affectionate and companionable cat, which can be very chatty with its owner. Sokokes are active cats that enjoy climbing.

🐾 **GROOMING** Regular stroking is all that is needed to keep the coat in good condition.

The Sokoke was discovered in Africa as recently as 1978. Its natural habitat is the Sokoke Forest of eastern Kenya—from which it takes its name. Its striped markings lend it the appearance of a wild cat such as an ocelot, and it may be that the Sokoke represents a previously undiscovered subspecies of cat.

The Sokoke first came to light when Jeni Slater, a Danish artist, found some specimens on her Kenyan coconut plantation. She has left a first-hand account of her strange discovery. "My gardener came to me one morning and reported some strange kittens with a mother born in a hollow under a tree in my garden. I went to investigate, and saw these huge eyes and big ears, and long tail erect and a smallish head with beautiful body markings. I knew immediately that this was something unusual and I therefore took a pair from the litter. With the help of the house staff I hand reared them."

The markings to which Slater refers are the pattern now known as "African Tabby." The look of it is similar to the classic blotched tabby pattern, and it is usually described as resembling wood-grain. How the Sokoke came by its stripes is a vexed question. Equally problematic is the

conundrum of its presence in the Sokoke Forest. Proponents of the breed are sure that it evolved there naturally, and claim that the cat is often spoken of in the lore of the local Giriama tribe. Others say that the cat is most likely descended from the pets of European settlers: that is, they are domestic cats that turned feral, and their strange coat is simply a genetic mutation. A compromise theory avers that the Sokoke is the result of interbreeding between domestic cats and wild ones.

Whatever their provenance, the first Sokokes proved surprisingly easy to tame. A pair was taken to Denmark by Jeni Slater's friend Gloria Moeldrup, and were shown in Copenhagen in 1984. That pair subsequently became the founders of a breeding program. The breed was recognized by the international cat association FIFé in 1993.

**ESSENTIALS**

SIZE

COAT CARE

ACTIVENESS

FRIENDLINESS

PLAYFULNESS

**EARS** Medium-large ears that are broad at the base with slightly rounded, tufted tips. They are set quite high on the head.

**EYES** Large, wide-set eyes that are slightly slanted. They are amber or light green in color.

**COLOR** The ground (background) color is sandy, and the pattern can range from very light brown to almost black. There are no white hairs.

**COAT** Very short, slightly shiny, close-lying coat with little or no undercoat.

**HEAD** Modified, wedge-shaped head that is flat between the ears. The high cheekbones are prominent, and the medium-length nose is straight, with nose leather of brick red outlined in the same color as the pattern on the coat.

**TAIL** Long, thin, whiplike tail.

**LEGS** The back legs are slightly longer than the front ones, and give the cat the appearance of being on tiptoe.

**PAWS** Oval-shaped paws with black or seal paw pads.

# Sable Burmese

## SABLE BURMESE FACTS

**PHYSIQUE** A medium-sized, muscular cat with a straight rather than an arched back. The American Burmese has a compact body, while the European Burmese is a more slender shape.

**COAT** Sable, or brown, is the original Burmese color. It is actually genetically black. It is one of four colors recognized for the American Burmese. The European Burmese comes in six solid colors, plus tortie colors.

**TEMPERAMENT** The Burmese is a companionable and adaptable cat that is renowned for its intelligent and pleasant nature.

**GROOMING** This cat benefits from regular brushing or stroking with a chamois-type cloth.

Known for 600 years, the Burmese was in fact never confined to Burma, but was found all over southeast Asia. Burmese cats were held to be sacred and (it is believed) were often resident in Buddhist temples. They were called "supalak" or "copper-colored"—a somewhat unlikely decription of their dark brown coat, which is known as sable in the United States and brown in the UK.

The Thai Cat-Book Poems, written some time between 1350 and 1767, characterizes the breed we now know as the Burmese as being "of magnificent appearance with shape the best, colored like copper, this cat is beautiful. The light of her eyes is as a shining ray." The founder of the modern breed was a brown female named Wong Mau, which was brought to the United States under obscure circumstances in 1930. In the United States, she was mated with a Seal Point Siamese. It was clear from the litters that Wong Mau produced that she must have some Siamese blood—she was what would now be called a Tonkinese. But the second and third generations of her offspring were back-crossed to isolate the gene that produced the allover brown coloring of the classic Burmese cat. Nearly all modern Burmese are derived from that base stock. The breed was recognized in the United States in 1936. But recognition was controversially withdrawn in 1941 due to disagreements within the cat-breeding community about the level of cross-breeding with Siamese. The Burmese breed was reinstated in 1953, but for many years only the original sable color was accepted. Today, three other colors—blue, champagne, and platinum—are also recognized. British breeders imported their first Burmese from the United States in 1947. They produced the cat in a wider range of colors. Moreover, British authorities favored a slightly different body shape: lighter, slimmer, and altogether more Siamese in character. These local differences have led to the establishment of two separate Burmese types. The American Cat Fanciers' Association (CFA) now recognizes both the American Burmese and the European Burmese. Both are highly popular cats, consistently ranking as one of the top registered breeds. Burmese cats are highly sociable creatures, and their extreme liking for company has led to them being dubbed "velcro cats."

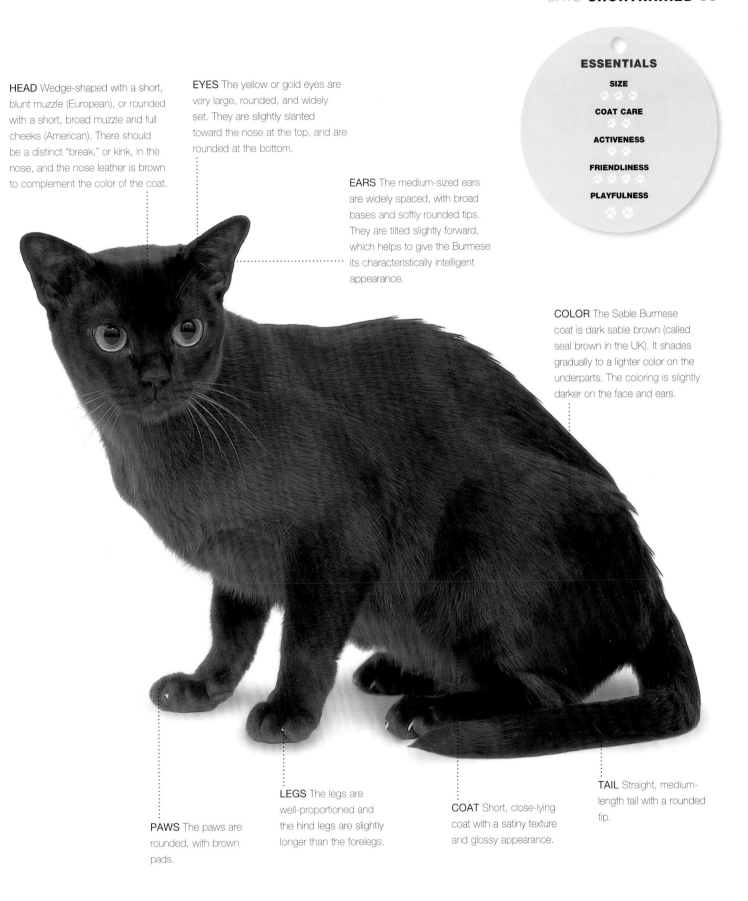

**HEAD** Wedge-shaped with a short, blunt muzzle (European), or rounded with a short, broad muzzle and full cheeks (American). There should be a distinct "break," or kink, in the nose, and the nose leather is brown to complement the color of the coat.

**EYES** The yellow or gold eyes are very large, rounded, and widely set. They are slightly slanted toward the nose at the top, and are rounded at the bottom.

**EARS** The medium-sized ears are widely spaced, with broad bases and softly rounded tips. They are tilted slightly forward, which helps to give the Burmese its characteristically intelligent appearance.

**ESSENTIALS**

SIZE

COAT CARE

ACTIVENESS

FRIENDLINESS

PLAYFULNESS

**COLOR** The Sable Burmese coat is dark sable brown (called seal brown in the UK). It shades gradually to a lighter color on the underparts. The coloring is slightly darker on the face and ears.

**PAWS** The paws are rounded, with brown pads.

**LEGS** The legs are well-proportioned and the hind legs are slightly longer than the forelegs.

**COAT** Short, close-lying coat with a satiny texture and glossy appearance.

**TAIL** Straight, medium-length tail with a rounded tip.

# Blue Burmese

## BLUE BURMESE FACTS

**PHYSIQUE** A medium-sized, muscular cat with a straight rather than an arched back. The American Burmese has a compact body, while the European Burmese is a more slender shape.

**COAT** Blue is one of four colors recognized for the American Burmese. The European Burmese comes in six solid colors, plus tortie colors.

**TEMPERAMENT** The Burmese is a companionable and adaptable cat that is renowned for its intelligent and pleasant nature.

**GROOMING** This cat benefits from regular brushing or stroking with a chamois-type cloth.

When breeders began to show Burmese in colors other than the original Sable, they were at first judged as "Mandalays" by the Cat Fanciers' Association. But in 1984, the CFA relaxed its stance and accepted the new Blue, Platinum, and Champagne varieties as Burmese. Other authorities allowed the lighter colors much earlier.

**COLOR** The coat is blue-gray, gradually shading to a lighter color on the underparts. The coloring is slightly darker on the face and ears. There should be warm fawn undertones in the American Burmese, while the European cat should be silvery.

**EARS** The medium-sized ears are widely spaced, with broad bases and softly rounded tips. They are tilted slightly forward, which give the Burmese its intelligent appearance.

**HEAD** Wedge-shaped with a short, blunt muzzle (European), or rounded with a short, broad muzzle and full cheeks (American). There should be a distinct "break," or kink, in the nose, with slate or dark gray leather to complement the color of the coat.

**TAIL** Straight, medium-length tail with a rounded tip.

**EYES** The yellow or gold eyes are very large, rounded, and widely set. They are slightly slanted toward the nose at the top, and rounded at the bottom.

**LEGS** The legs are well-proportioned and the hind legs are slightly longer than the forelegs.

**COAT** Short, close-lying coat with a satiny texture and glossy appearance.

**PAWS** The paws are rounded, with pinkish-gray pads (slate-gray pads are also acceptable in the American Burmese).

### ESSENTIALS

**SIZE**
🐾 🐾 🐾

**COAT CARE**
🐾

**ACTIVENESS**
🐾 🐾

**FRIENDLINESS**
🐾 🐾 🐾 🐾

**PLAYFULNESS**
🐾 🐾

# Champagne Burmese

This cat is paler than the original Sable Burmese, as the American term Champagne attests. The fur is a warm, milk-chocolate in color. Breeders aim for an even color, but the Burmese coat is slightly lighter on the underparts and may be darker on the ears and face—a vestige of its Siamese heritage.

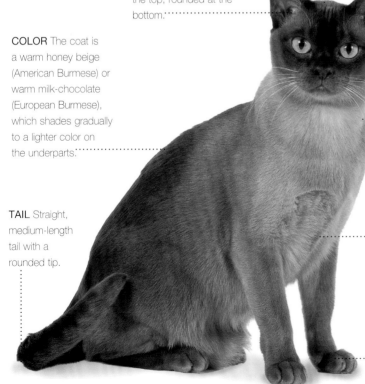

**HEAD** Wedge-shaped with a short, blunt muzzle (European), or rounded with a short, broad muzzle and full cheeks (American). There is a distinct "break," or kink, in the nose, which has chocolate-brown nose leather.

**EYES** The yellow or gold eyes are very large, rounded, and widely set. They are slightly slanted towards the nose at the top, rounded at the bottom.

**EARS** Medium-sized and widely spaced, with broad bases and softly rounded tips. They are tilted slightly forward, which gives an intelligent appearance.

**COLOR** The coat is a warm honey beige (American Burmese) or warm milk-chocolate (European Burmese), which shades gradually to a lighter color on the underparts.

**COAT** Short, close-lying coat with a satiny texture and glossy appearance.

**LEGS** The legs are well-proportioned and the hind legs are slightly longer than the forelegs.

**TAIL** Straight, medium-length tail with a rounded tip.

**PAWS** The paws are rounded, with pads that are pinkish tan for the American cat, cinnamon shading to chocolate-brown for the European cat.

## CHAMPAGNE BURMESE FACTS

**PHYSIQUE** A medium-sized, muscular cat with a straight rather than an arched back. The American Burmese has a compact body, while the European Burmese is a more slender shape.

**COAT** Champagne is one of four colors recognized for the American Burmese. The color is more widely known as chocolate and it is one of six solid colors accepted for the European Burmese, which also comes in tortie colors.

**TEMPERAMENT** The Burmese is a companionable and adaptable cat that is renowned for its intelligent and pleasant nature.

**GROOMING** This cat benefits from regular brushing or stroking with a chamois-type cloth.

### ESSENTIALS

SIZE

COAT CARE

ACTIVENESS

FRIENDLINESS

PLAYFULNESS

# Platinum (Lilac) Burmese

## PLATINUM (LILAC) BURMESE FACTS

**PHYSIQUE** A medium-sized, muscular cat with a straight rather than an arched back. The American Burmese has a compact body, while the European Burmese is a more slender shape..

**COAT** Platinum is one of four colors recognized for the American Burmese. The color is more widely known as lilac and it is one of six solid colors accepted for the European Burmese, which also comes in tortoiseshell colors.

**TEMPERAMENT** The Burmese is a companionable and adaptable cat that is renowned for its intelligent and pleasant nature.

**GROOMING** This cat benefits from regular brushing or stroking with a chamois-type cloth.

Occasionally, a brown Burmese would produce kittens of a lighter color, which were then bred to recreate the more delicate shades. The Platinum (Lilac) Burmese is a dilute form of the Champagne (Chocolate). Both the platinum and champagne colors became established in the 1970s, but were not recognized in the United States for another decade.

**HEAD** Wedge-shaped with a short, blunt muzzle (European), or rounded with a short, broad muzzle and full cheeks (American). There should be a distinct "break," or kink, in the nose, and the nose leather is lavender-pink to complement the color of the coat.

**EYES** The yellow or gold eyes are very large, rounded, and widely set. They are slightly slanted toward the nose at the top, and rounded at the bottom.

**EARS** The medium-sized ears are widely spaced, with broad bases and softly rounded tips. They are tilted slightly forward, which helps to give the Burmese its characteristically intelligent appearance.

**COLOR** The coat is described as pale silvery-gray with fawn undertones (American) or dove-gray with a pinkish cast (European), which shades gradually to a lighter color on the underparts.

**LEGS** The legs are well-proportioned and the hind legs are slightly longer than the forelegs.

**COAT** Short, close-lying coat with a satiny texture and glossy appearance.

**PAWS** The paws are rounded, with lavender-pink pads.

**TAIL** Straight, medium-length tail with a rounded tip.

**ESSENTIALS**

SIZE

COAT CARE

ACTIVENESS

FRIENDLINESS

PLAYFULNESS

# Red Burmese

Breeders aiming to extend the color range of the Burmese welcomed the introduction of the red gene, which made red, cream, and tortie Burmese possible. The Red Burmese coat is a warm tangerine hue, much lighter than that of other red cats. There may be slight tabby markings on the face.

## RED BURMESE FACTS

**PHYSIQUE** A medium-sized, muscular cat with a straight rather than an arched back. The American Burmese has a compact body, while the European Burmese is a more slender shape..

**COAT** Red is one of six solid colors accepted for the European Burmese, which also comes in tortoiseshell colors.

**TEMPERAMENT** The Burmese is a companionable and adaptable cat that is renowned for its intelligent and pleasant nature.

**GROOMING** This cat benefits from regular brushing or stroking with a chamois-type cloth.

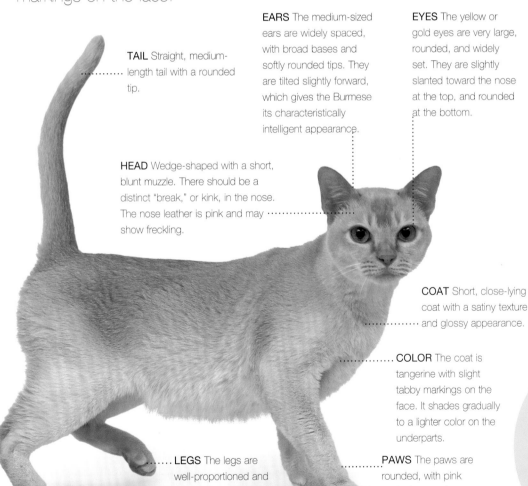

**TAIL** Straight, medium-length tail with a rounded tip.

**EARS** The medium-sized ears are widely spaced, with broad bases and softly rounded tips. They are tilted slightly forward, which gives the Burmese its characteristically intelligent appearance.

**EYES** The yellow or gold eyes are very large, rounded, and widely set. They are slightly slanted toward the nose at the top, and rounded at the bottom.

**HEAD** Wedge-shaped with a short, blunt muzzle. There should be a distinct "break," or kink, in the nose. The nose leather is pink and may show freckling.

**COAT** Short, close-lying coat with a satiny texture and glossy appearance.

**COLOR** The coat is tangerine with slight tabby markings on the face. It shades gradually to a lighter color on the underparts.

**LEGS** The legs are well-proportioned and the hind legs are slightly longer than the forelegs.

**PAWS** The paws are rounded, with pink pads that may have some freckling.

**ESSENTIALS**

SIZE

COAT CARE

ACTIVENESS

FRIENDLINESS

PLAYFULNESS

# Cream Burmese

## CREAM BURMESE FACTS

**PHYSIQUE** A medium-sized, muscular cat with a straight rather than an arched back. The American Burmese has a compact body, while the European Burmese is a more slender shape.

**COAT** Cream is one of six solid colors accepted for the European Burmese, which also comes in tortoiseshell colors.

**TEMPERAMENT** The Burmese is a companionable and adaptable cat that is renowned for its intelligent and pleasant nature. It needs plenty of attention, and regular playtime.

**GROOMING** This cat benefits from regular brushing or stroking with a chamois-type cloth.

Cream—which is a dilute version of red—is an acceptable coat color for the European Burmese, but not for the American Burmese. Both shades were recognized by European authorities in the 1970s. The perfect show Burmese has eyes that are golden rather than yellow, and these perfectly complement the rich tone of the cream coat.

**COLOR** The coat is light apricot with a powdery bloom on the back, top of the head, and the ears. There may be slight tabby markings on the face. It shades gradually to a lighter color on the underparts.

**HEAD** Wedge-shaped with a short, blunt muzzle. There should be a distinct "break," or kink, in the nose. The nose leather is pink and may show freckling.

**EARS** The medium-sized ears are widely spaced, with broad bases and softly rounded tips. They are tilted slightly forward, which helps to give an intelligent appearance.

**EYES** The eyes are very large, rounded, and widely set. Yellow or gold is desirable but colors may vary. They are slightly slanted toward the nose at the top, and rounded at the bottom.

**TAIL** Straight, medium-length tail with a rounded tip.

## ESSENTIALS

**SIZE**

**COAT CARE**

**ACTIVENESS**

**FRIENDLINESS**

**PLAYFULNESS**

**COAT** Short, close-lying coat with a satiny texture and glossy appearance.

**LEGS** The legs are well-proportioned and the hind legs are slightly longer than the forelegs.

**PAWS** The paws are rounded, with pink pads that may be slightly freckled.

# Tortoiseshell Burmese

Tortie Burmese, introduced in the 1970s, are the result of crossing Reds or Creams with Browns, Blues, Chocolates, or Lilacs. The colors can form distinct blotches or be softly intermingled, and blazes or solid legs and tails are permitted. Since red and cream are not recognized for the American Burmese, neither are the tortoiseshell colors.

**HEAD** Wedge-shaped with a short, blunt muzzle. There should be a distinct "break," or kink, in the nose. The plain or blotched nose leather complements the coat color.

**EARS** The medium-sized ears are widely spaced, with broad bases and softly rounded tips. They are tilted slightly forward, which helps to give a characteristically intelligent appearance.

**COLOR** The coat features a main color, with shades of red or cream. It shades gradually to a lighter color on the underparts.

**LEGS** The legs are well-proportioned and the hind legs are slightly longer than the forelegs.

**TAIL** Straight, medium-length tail with a rounded tip.

**PAWS** The paws are rounded, with plain or blotched pads that harmonize with the color of the coat.

**EYES** The yellow or gold eyes are very large, rounded, and widely set. They are slightly slanted toward the nose at the top, and rounded at the bottom.

**COAT** Short, close-lying coat with a satiny texture and glossy appearance.

## TORTOISESHELL BURMESE FACTS

**PHYSIQUE** A medium-sized, muscular cat with a straight rather than an arched back. The American Burmese has a compact body, while the European Burmese is a more slender shape.

**COAT** There are four recognized tortoiseshell colors for the European Burmese: brown tortie, blue tortie, chocolate tortie, and lilac tortie.

**TEMPERAMENT** The Burmese is a companionable and adaptable cat that is renowned for its intelligent and pleasant nature. It needs plenty of attention, and regular playtime.

**GROOMING** This cat benefits from regular brushing or stroking with a chamois-type cloth.

### ESSENTIALS

**SIZE**

**COAT CARE**

**ACTIVENESS**

**FRIENDLINESS**

**PLAYFULNESS**

# Bombay

## BOMBAY FACTS

**PHYSIQUE** This is a slender, muscular cat with a straight back and long, slim legs.

**COAT** As well as the black Bombay, the Asian Self comes in blue, chocolate, lilac, red, cream, caramel, and apricot, in standard and silvered versions. The same colors (except for apricot) are accepted as tortie colors.

**TEMPERAMENT** An even-tempered, dignified cat, the Bombay makes a loving companion, and needs attention.

**GROOMING** Occasional brushing is all that is needed to keep the coat looking good.

Prized for its coal-black coat, the striking Bombay is also known as the Black Asian Self. It is one of the so-called "Asian Group" of cats, which also includes the Burmilla and the Tiffanie. The British Bombay is often confused with an American cat of the same name, which is a cross between the Burmese and the American Shorthair.

The American version of the Bombay came first. It was created by Nikki Horner, a breeder from Louisville, Kentucky who wanted to engineer a Burmese with a jet-black coat. The cat which resulted from her program was, she said proudly, "a copper-eyed mini-panther with patent-leather fur." The name Bombay was an oblique reference to the Indian black panther. The American-bred Bombay—sometimes described as "a parlor-panther"—was perhaps the first cat bred specifically to emulate in miniature the look of a wild feline species. Others followed: the Ocicat (which is intended to look like an ocelot), the Pixiebob (bobcat), the California Spangled (leopard), and the Toyger (tiger). The British Bombay came about in the 1980s. It belongs to the "Asian group"—a set of cats that are Burmese in type, but come in a range of coats and patterns (and, in the case of the Tiffanie, coat length). We might say that the relationship of the Burmese to the Asian group is analogous to the relationship of the Siamese to Oriental Shorthairs, which are Siamese in type but differently colored and patterned. All the members of the Asian group share a common Burmese heritage, but in the eyes of the UK's Governing Council of the Cat Fancy, they are distinct enough to constitute more than a single breed. The Black was one of the original self varieties of the Asian group, which helps to explain why it came to have an evocative name rather than a merely descriptive one. In the UK, Bombays are by definition shorthaired, but semi-longhaired versions of the Bombay are recognized by some registries. Black is the only permissible color for the Bombay which, like its American counterpart, should have a coat that lies close to the body, producing its spectacular patent-leather sheen.

**ESSENTIALS**

SIZE

COAT CARE

ACTIVENESS

FRIENDLINESS

PLAYFULNESS

**EARS** Medium to large, broad-based ears with rounded tips. They are set well apart and are tilted slightly forward.

**EYES** Medium to large, wide-set, expressive eyes. They may be yellow through to green, but gold is the ideal color.

**HEAD** Short wedge with a distinct "break," or kink, in the nose and a blunt muzzle. The nose is straight and the tip aligns with the tip of the chin. The nose leather is solid black.

**TAIL** Medium to long tail with a rounded tip.

**COAT** Short, fine, close-lying coat that should be smooth to the touch and glossy in appearance.

**LEGS** Long, slender legs that end in neat, oval paws. The paw pads are black or dark brown.

# Burmilla (Asian Shaded)

## BURMILLA FACTS

**PHYSIQUE** Slender, muscular cat with a straight back, rounded chest, and long, slim legs.

**COAT** The Burmilla can be heavily shaded or lightly tipped with color. It comes in black, brown, blue, chocolate, lilac, red, cream, caramel, or apricot, and also in the silver versions of these colors.

**TEMPERAMENT** An even-tempered, loving cat.

**GROOMING** Occasional brushing is all that is needed.

The elegant Burmilla, or Asian Shaded, is one of the many breeds that came about by accident, only to be carried forward by a professional breeder.

But in this instance, the progenitors of the Burmilla, or Asian Shaded, were themselves pedigree cats. The Burmilla has its origins, as its name suggests, in a cross between a Burmese and a Chinchilla.

The Burmilla is the original variety of the Asian group. It was created by a British breeder named Baroness Miranda von Kirchberg. Among the cats that she owned were a male silver Chinchilla named Sanquist and a female Burmese named Fabergé, each of which were due to be mated to one of their own breed. When Fabergé came into season, she was locked in a room for the night before her journey to the stud. But unbeknownst to von Kirchberg, the door was opened by a cleaner who heard the cat mewing unhappily, and did not know why it had been isolated. Fabergé was mated to a Burmese as planned, but when her four kittens were born they were not purebred Burmese. They were good Burmese types, but had the shaded silver coats of a Chinchilla. The only possible explanation was that Fabergé had found her way to

Sanquist, and was already pregnant when she went to stud. The four kitttens were named Gabriella, Galatea, Gemma, and Gisella. Normally, they would have been neutered and given away as pets. But they were exceptionally beautiful, and it seemed a shame to dispose of them. More than that, Baroness von Kirchberg realized immediately that they provided an opportunity to fill a gap: they could be used to breed silver and tabby Burmese. After consulting with geneticists and the UK's Governing Council of the Cat Fancy (GCCF), Baroness von Kirchberg embarked on a breeding program and formed a Burmilla Association. A breeder named Therese Clarke acquired Gemma from the original litter and in 1984 began the Burmilla Cat Club. She also published a newsletter with the punning title of BCC Mews. All these efforts paid off, as the Burmilla achieved GCCF championship status in 1997—a matter of months after Baroness von Kirchberg died.

**ESSENTIALS**

SIZE

COAT CARE

ACTIVENESS

FRIENDLINESS

PLAYFULNESS

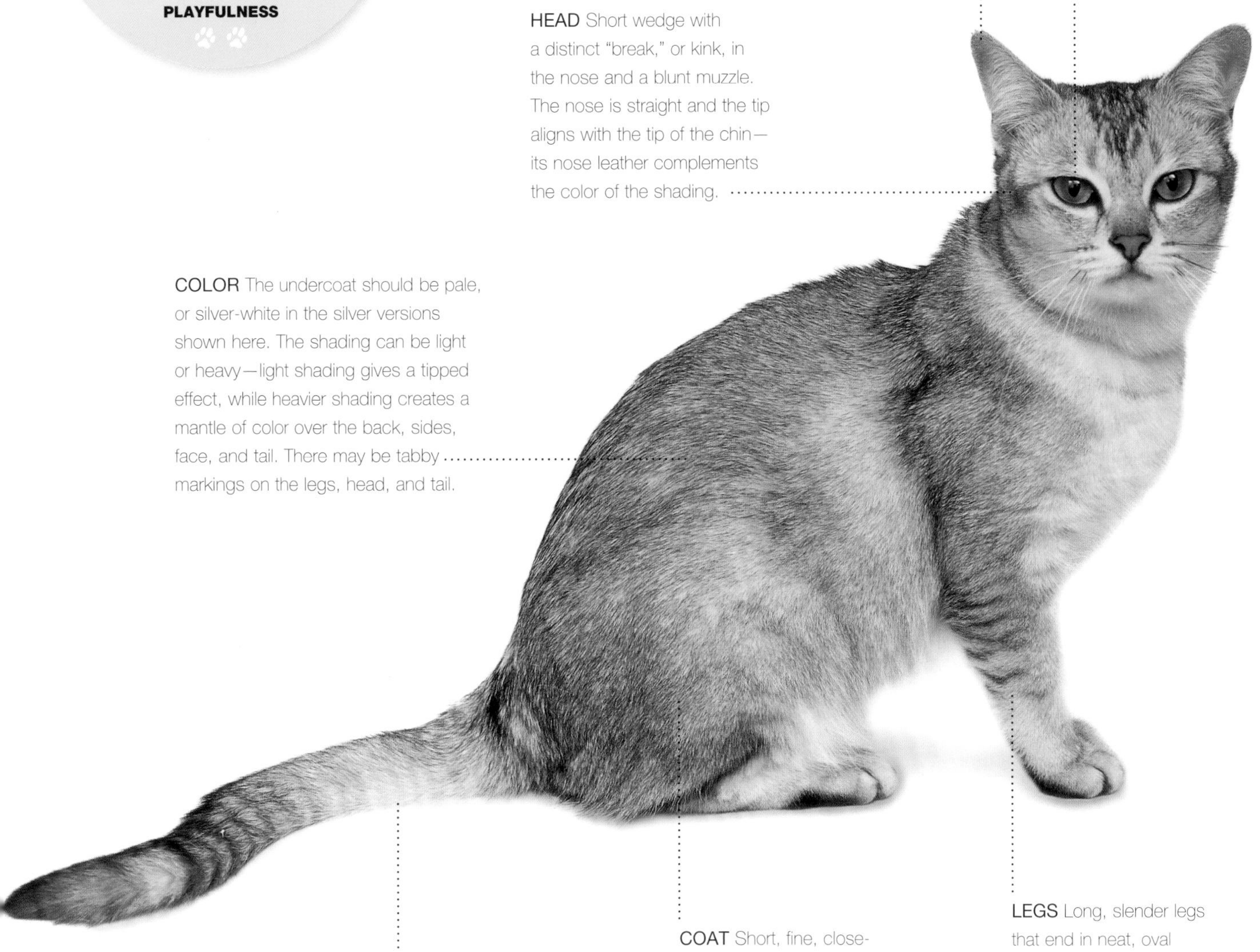

**EARS** Medium to large, broad-based ears that have rounded tips. They are set well apart and are tilted slightly forward.

**EYES** Medium to large, wide-set, expressive eyes that are rimmed with black. They may be yellow through to green— gold is the ideal color.

**HEAD** Short wedge with a distinct "break," or kink, in the nose and a blunt muzzle. The nose is straight and the tip aligns with the tip of the chin— its nose leather complements the color of the shading.

**COLOR** The undercoat should be pale, or silver-white in the silver versions shown here. The shading can be light or heavy—light shading gives a tipped effect, while heavier shading creates a mantle of color over the back, sides, face, and tail. There may be tabby markings on the legs, head, and tail.

**TAIL** Medium to long tail with a rounded tip.

**COAT** Short, fine, close-lying coat that should be smooth to the touch and glossy in appearance.

**LEGS** Long, slender legs that end in neat, oval paws. The paw pads complement the color of the coat.

# Asian Smoke

## ASIAN SMOKE FACTS

**PHYSIQUE** Slender, muscular cat with a straight back and gently rounded chest. The legs are long, slim, and elegant.

**COAT** The Asian Smoke comes in the same colors as the Burmilla (Asian Shaded). The undercoat is silver-white or near-white.

**TEMPERAMENT** An even-tempered, dignified cat. The Asian Smoke makes a loving companion, and needs attention.

**GROOMING** Occasional brushing is all that is needed to keep the coat looking good.

The Asian Smoke was once called the Burmoire. It should look like a solidly colored cat when it is in repose and reveal its pale undercoat when it moves. It may have ghost tabby markings on its head, legs, and tail, giving the coat the appearance of watered silk.

There are four varieties in the Asian shorthair group, including the Asian Smoke. The other varieties are the Asian Tabby, the Asian Self (including the Bombay) and the Burmilla. This particular variation was developed first in Britain in 1981 by accident, when Baroness Miranda von Kirchberg crossed a Chinchilla with a Lilac Burmese. The litter of four kittens was used to breed the first of the Asian cats.

This slender cat comes in a range of colors including black, blue, caramel tortoiseshell, chocolate, black, and cream. Often the Smoke has an undercoat of white or silver, so even though the cat appears to be a solid color it can show flashes of white when it moves or the hair is tufted backwards. The tail should be straight and medium length; if there is a kink in the tail this is considered a fault and will not be accepted for showing.

This elegant cat has a slim, muscular build with a compact body and hind legs that are slightly taller than the shoulders. This breed is intelligent and outgoing and is known to be friendly although it is a fairly vocal cat, which will demand the attention of its owner. Like the Burmese, these cats like affection including being held and like to play. They have a lot of energy, are quite inquisitive and will explore its surroundings.

**COLOR** The pale undercoat should constitute no less than one-third and no more than one-half of the total hair length. There may be silver "clown markings"—frown marks on the forehead and rings round the eyes.

**ESSENTIALS**

SIZE

COAT CARE

ACTIVENESS

FRIENDLINESS

PLAYFULNESS

**HEAD** Short wedge with a distinct "break," or kink, in the nose and a blunt muzzle. The nose is straight and the tip aligns with the tip of the chin. The nose leather complements the color of the coat.

**EARS** Medium to large, broad-based ears that have rounded tips. They are set well apart and are tilted slightly forward.

**COAT** Short, fine, close-lying coat that should be smooth to the touch and glossy in appearance.

**TAIL** Medium to long tail with a rounded tip.

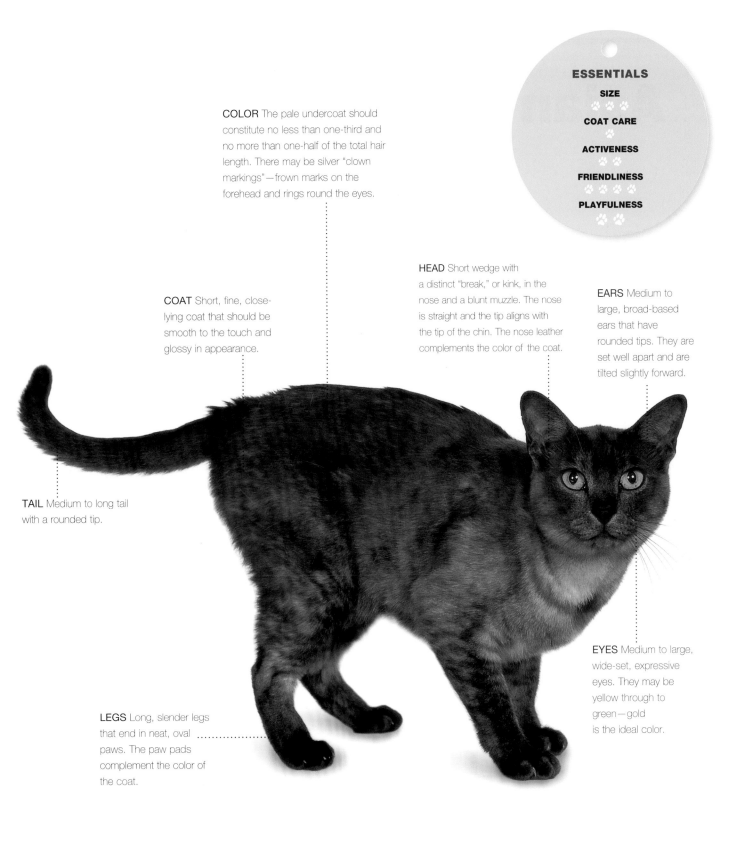

**EYES** Medium to large, wide-set, expressive eyes. They may be yellow through to green—gold is the ideal color.

**LEGS** Long, slender legs that end in neat, oval paws. The paw pads complement the color of the coat.

# Asian Tabby

## ASIAN TABBY FACTS

**PHYSIQUE** Slender, muscular cat with a straight back, gently rounded chest, and long, slim legs.

**COAT** All four tabby patterns (classic, mackerel, spotted, and ticked) are recognized. The Asian Tabby comes in the same colors as the Burmilla.

**TEMPERAMENT** An even-tempered, dignified cat. The Asian Tabby makes a loving companion, and needs attention.

**GROOMING** Occasional brushing is all that is needed.

The Asian Tabby is one of the few cats recognized in all four tabby patterns in the UK. Asian Tabbies are still relatively uncommon; the most popular of the four types is the Ticked Tabby, which was achieved by introducing the Abyssinian into the breeding program. The Asian Tabbies come in all the Asian group colors.

The tabby can be spotted, classic, mackerel or ticked and each has a definitive 'm' on the forehead just above the eyes. Like other Asians, this breed is accepted in many colors such as black, blue, chocolate, lilac, caramel, red, cream, apricot, tortoiseshell, silver shaded, and silver standard. A strong pattern is always desired for showing these cats. The most common Asian Tabby is the 'ticked' variety; however breeders are currently working to achieve highly defined patterning on the other three varieties to increase their popularity.

This cat is even-tempered and makes a loving companion. Asian breeds are renowned for their gentle, easy-going attitude; they will be playful, affectionate and greatly enjoy being with their owner. Good with children, these cats make wonderful family pets that are easy to maintain – occasional brushing should suffice to keep the coat in good condition.

These cats are well-behaved travellers and will sit quite happily in a cat carrier, although they are inquisitive cats and will explore new surroundings. The behaviour is likened to the Burmese; they like the attention of the owner and like to be held and cuddled. The Asian Tabby can be quite vocal too, and they have loud voices when they want something. Energetic for life, these cats are reliable and great with people.

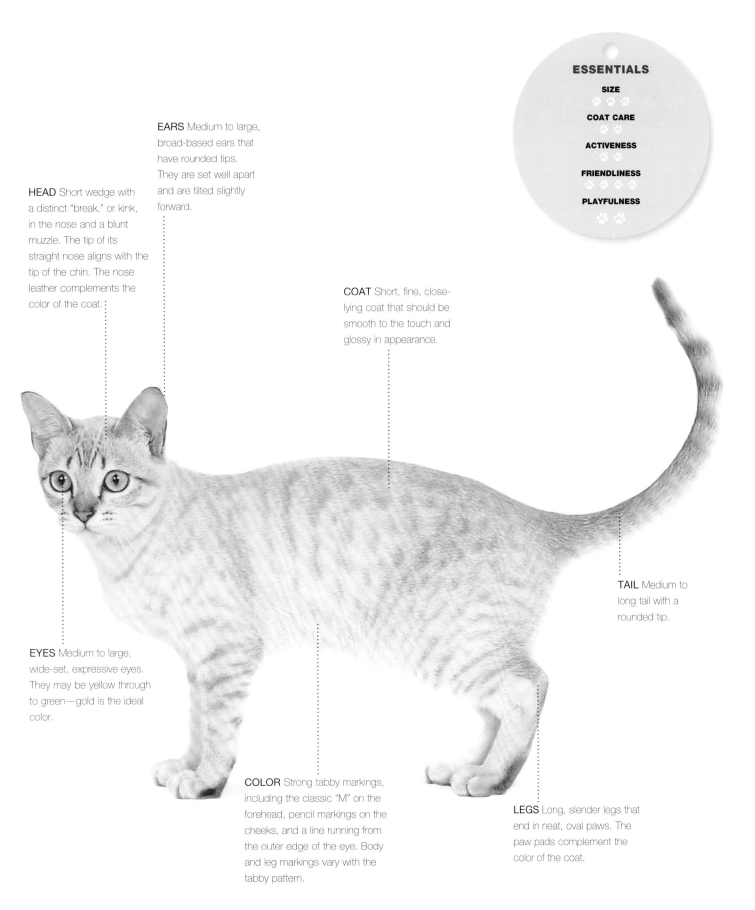

**ESSENTIALS**

SIZE

COAT CARE

ACTIVENESS

FRIENDLINESS

PLAYFULNESS

**EARS** Medium to large, broad-based ears that have rounded tips. They are set well apart and are tilted slightly forward.

**HEAD** Short wedge with a distinct "break," or kink, in the nose and a blunt muzzle. The tip of its straight nose aligns with the tip of the chin. The nose leather complements the color of the coat.

**COAT** Short, fine, close-lying coat that should be smooth to the touch and glossy in appearance.

**TAIL** Medium to long tail with a rounded tip.

**EYES** Medium to large, wide-set, expressive eyes. They may be yellow through to green—gold is the ideal color.

**COLOR** Strong tabby markings, including the classic "M" on the forehead, pencil markings on the cheeks, and a line running from the outer edge of the eye. Body and leg markings vary with the tabby pattern.

**LEGS** Long, slender legs that end in neat, oval paws. The paw pads complement the color of the coat.

# Chartreux

## CHARTREUX FACTS

**PHYSIQUE** A large, robust, muscular cat with quite short, fine-boned legs. The build is neither "cobby" nor slender, but has been described as "primitive." Males of this breed are much larger than females.

**COAT** The Chartreux cat comes only in blue-gray, with light silvering at the tips.

**TEMPERAMENT** This breed is reserved and undemanding, but can make a devoted pet. They are excellent hunters. Many Chartreux do not meow, but some make a chirping sound.

**GROOMING** Occasional grooming is all that is needed.

The blue-gray Chartreux has, for centuries, been associated with the monastery of Grande Chartreuse near Grenoble in France. But like many of the stories linking particular cats with religious institutions, this is almost certainly a myth. Yet the sweet-tempered Chartreux is without doubt a French native, and may once have been France's most common breed of cat.

The archives of the Grande Chartreuse make no mention of the blue cat that is supposed to have been a fixture inside its walls throughout the Middle Ages. The earliest reference to the breed is in a book written at the beginning of the 18th century by a French naturalist named Buffon, in which he called it "the cat of France." About 50 years later, an English encyclopedist named George Howard stated confidently that "in France the cats are all of a bluish-lead color." This was surely an exaggeration, but it does suggest that the Chartreux is descended from a common strain among French streets cats. As for the Chartreux name, the most likely explanation is that it derives from pile de Chartreux, the old French term for a kind of Spanish wool, the texture of which is believed to have resembled the Chartreux's thick coat.

The numbers of Chartreux dwindled over the decades to the point of extinction. French breeders began to take a serious interest in the cat in the 1920s and 1930s, but the Second World War damaged its chances of survival. Nevertheless, at that time it became a kind of patriotic symbol of France: Charles de Gaulle owned a Chartreux, and the writer Colette had two. After the war, the breed was revived through outcrossing to British Blue Shorthairs; for a while the two breeds were practically identical. As a result the Chartreux is not recognized in the UK.

But the Chartreux recovered its distinct identity, and is recognized by all the major registries outside the UK. It is the subject of one strange recent tradition: all the pedigree cats born in a calendar year have official names beginning with the same letter: "T" for 2002, "U" for 2003—and so on.

**ESSENTIALS**

SIZE

COAT CARE

ACTIVENESS

FRIENDLINESS

PLAYFULNESS

**HEAD** Broad, rounded head with full cheeks, narrow muzzle, and a straight, medium-length nose with a slight kink at eye level. The nose leather is slate-gray. The neck is short and thick.

**EARS** Erect, medium-sized ears that are placed high on the head.

**EYES** The eyes are rounded and slightly slanted with a sweet expression. The color range is copper to gold; a clear, deep, brilliant orange is preferred.

**COLOR** Any shade of blue-gray is allowable. The hairs are silver-tipped, giving the cat a natural sheen.

**TAIL** Medium-length tail that is thick at the base and tapers to the rounded tip.

**COAT** Short to medium-length thick coat with a slightly woolly texture.

**LEGS** The legs are short but slender, with rounded paws. The pads are a shade of pink described as rose-taupe.

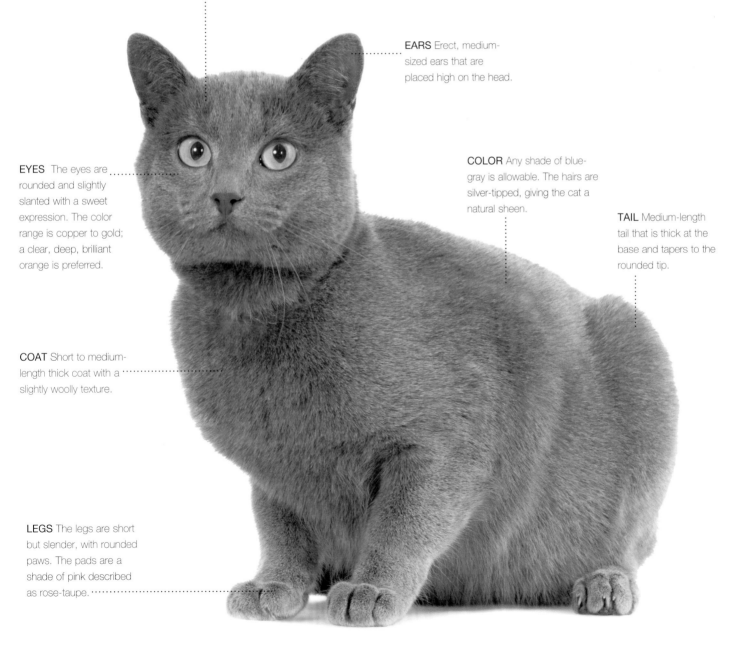

# Snowshoe

## SNOWSHOE FACTS

🐾 **PHYSIQUE** Medium to large cat that is well-balanced and extremely muscular.

🐾 **COAT** Some associations accept only Seal Point and Blue Point Snowshoes. Others accept all solid and tortie colors, and tabby patterns.

🐾 **TEMPERAMENT** These are active cats that are highly sociable and affectionate. They are vocal, but have much softer voices than their Siamese ancestors.

🐾 **GROOMING** Regular, gentle brushing is recommended to keep the coat well maintained.

The Snowshoe is an American breed, engineered in the 1960s with a view to combining the pointing of the Siamese with white feet like a Birman. The white extremities of the Snowshoe are its defining feature, but the permissible norm is broad: the spotting may extend along the leg, or may only cover the cat's toes.

White spotting on the paws was once a common defect in pedigree Siamese. It was diligently bred out over the years by Siamese breeders. But in the 1960s, an American breeder of Siamese, Dorothy Hinds-Daugherty of Philadelphia, found three spotted cats in a litter. She decided to take this fault and make a virtue of it. In the face of strong opposition from Siamese purists, she began a program to foster cats that had Siamese pointing, but which also sported little white boots.

The strongly contrasting pattern of the Snowshoe was achieved by outcrosssing Siamese with American Shorthairs and Birmans. This has resulted in a body that is rounder and broader than the Siamese archetype, but which should stop well short of "cobbiness." Some experts say that the Snowshoe's physique resembles that of the Siamese of half a century ago—before extreme angularity became the preferred type for today's Siamese.

Proponents of the breed claim that Snowshoes are like snowflakes: no two are ever alike. This is a fond way of saying that the pattern accepted for show is very hard to achieve. In the mitted pattern, the white is confined to the chin, chest, back legs, and paws—equating to about one-quarter of the cat. In the bicolor, the cat is up to half white. The white areas cover the legs, chest, and chin, with a white inverted "V" on the face—a feature described as the "Lone Ranger" look.

The Snowshoe breed is most commonly found in seal point and blue point, the black-based colors that provide the strongest contrast against the white spotting. But Red Point, Cream Point, and Lilac Point Snowshoes are among the variants.

**ESSENTIALS**

SIZE

COAT CARE

ACTIVENESS

FRIENDLINESS

PLAYFULNESS

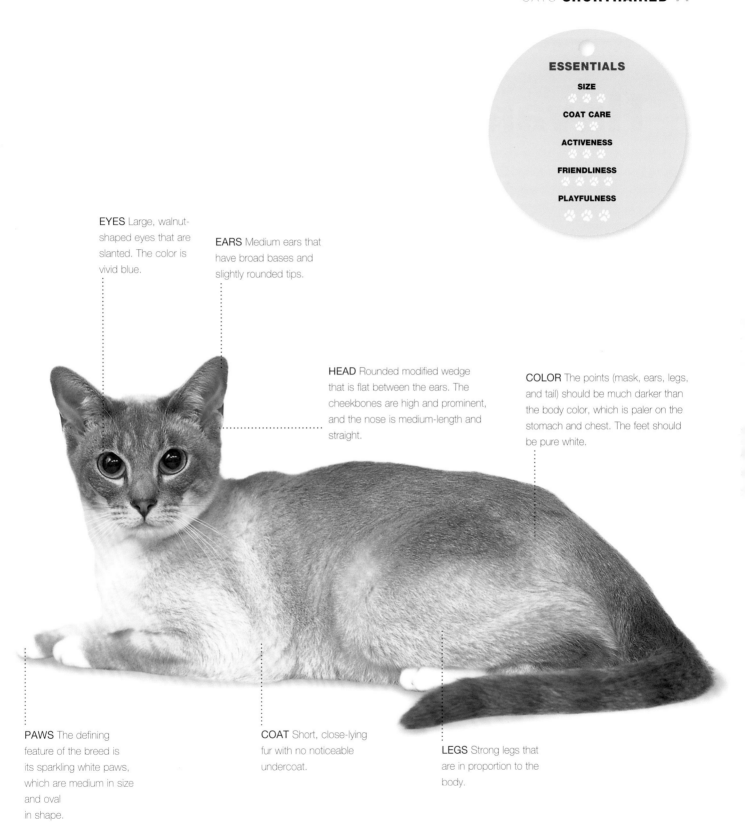

**EYES** Large, walnut-shaped eyes that are slanted. The color is vivid blue.

**EARS** Medium ears that have broad bases and slightly rounded tips.

**HEAD** Rounded modified wedge that is flat between the ears. The cheekbones are high and prominent, and the nose is medium-length and straight.

**COLOR** The points (mask, ears, legs, and tail) should be much darker than the body color, which is paler on the stomach and chest. The feet should be pure white.

**PAWS** The defining feature of the breed is its sparkling white paws, which are medium in size and oval in shape.

**COAT** Short, close-lying fur with no noticeable undercoat.

**LEGS** Strong legs that are in proportion to the body.

# Havana Brown

## HAVANA BROWN FACTS

**PHYSIQUE** A medium-sized, graceful cat with well-built muscles and surprising weight for its size.

**COAT** The coat is short-medium, although long-haired varieties do exist. The coat is soft and glossy and does come in two colors; brown and lilac. The brown tends to be a warm, rich shade.

**TEMPERAMENT** This cat is known for its loving personality and is very gentle, with a tendency to play. This cat does not do well left alone for prolonged periods, and craves human interaction.

**GROOMING** Regular, gentle brushing is recommended to keep the coat well maintained.

The Havana Brown was developed in the 1950s by a group of breeders who collaborated to cross self-brown cats with domestic black cats such as the black domestic Shorthair, chocolate point Siamese and Russian Blue cats. The breed varies from Britain to the US, with British varieties containing more Siamese, which are known as Chestnut Brown Oriental cats. It was in the US that the name 'Havana Brown' was coined, separating the two breeds.

The origins of the breed actually date back much further than the 50s, with the Siamese brown known in Siam (now Thailand) for centuries. Some of the first cats to be transported from Siam to Britain in the 19th century were brown, and when exhibited gained a lot of attention. The breed disappeared during World War Two, but was redeveloped in the 50s. Suggested by the name the Havana Brown is has a brown coat, and is the only breed that requires brown whiskers for the Kennel Club Pedigree. When the breed was first developed the coat was a rich chestnut, chocolaty shade but as standard it can range from a mahogany to a reddish brown – The International Cat Association accepts a wide range of browns for this breed. The breed is recognized by three organisations; the Cat Fancier's Association (CFA), the American Cat Fancier's Association (AFCA) and The International Cat Association (TICA). It is considered an endangered breed die to the low number of kittens produced each year. This is a very dependant breed that should not be left on its own for long periods of time. This cat craves the attention and time of its owner, and likes to be a part of all your activities. The Havana Brown is extremely gentle, affectionate and likes to play. If properly socialized, the cat will live happily with other pets and children and is a friendly and outgoing companion. A relaxed cat, the Havana Brown has a nice balance of activeness and down time and will adapt to any situation well.

A quiet cat, the Havana Brown needs very little grooming and the best care to give this cat is your attention. A medium sized cat with a short coat, it makes for a clean and well-behaved pet.

**EYES** The Havana Brown has beautiful green eyes that are alert and expressive, medium-sized and oval.

**EARS** The ears are wide-set and rounded at the tips, cupping slightly at the base.

**ESSENTIALS**

SIZE

COAT CARE

ACTIVENESS

FRIENDLINESS

PLAYFULNESS

**WHISKERS** The whiskers must be the same shade as the coat; white whiskers will discount the cat from show quality.

**HEAD** The Havana Brown's head is distinctly longer than it is wide, with a narrow muzzle – the shape of the head is a defining feature of the Havana Brown and must be correct in show-quality cats.

**LEGS** The legs are straight and tall, with females' legs being slimmer than the more muscular males.

**TAIL** The tail is medium in length and slender.

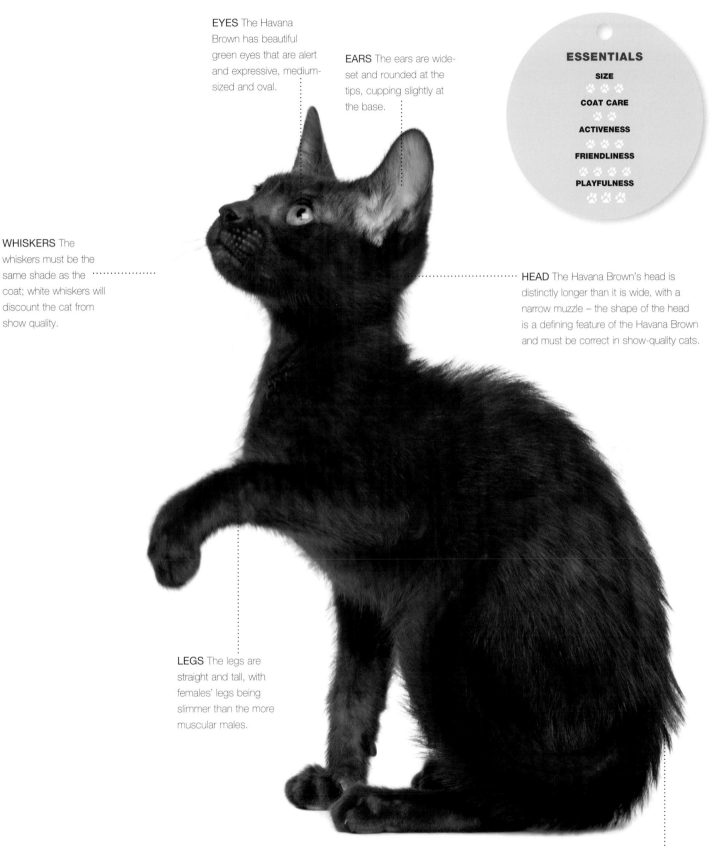

# Persians

The Persian is the archetypal longhaired cat, with beautiful fur that is long and flowing. Its coat is a double one, consisting of a woolly undercoat with a layer of long guard hairs on top. It needs thorough daily grooming (and regular bathing) to keep it free from tangles—a time-consuming task for the Persian owner. Persians are known officially as Longhairs in the UK, where each color is classed as a different breed. Elsewhere, different colors are seen as variants of the one breed. The Persian is the perfect "lap cat." It enjoys company and has a very placid, calm temperament.

# Black Persian

## BLACK PERSIAN FACTS

 **PHYSIQUE** A medium-large, heavy-boned, "cobby" cat with short, sturdy legs and a broad chest, back, and shoulders. The body's rounded appearance is enhanced by the fluffy coat.

 **COAT** The Persian comes in many colors and patterns. Black is one of seven recognized self (solid) colors.

 **TEMPERAMENT** This is a placid indoor cat with a sweet and responsive nature. The Persian enjoys play but is undemanding.

 **GROOMING** The Persian's coat needs thorough daily combing to keep it tangle-free.

Persians are distinguished by their thick, luxuriant coats and flat facial features. They are immensely popular worldwide, and they come in a huge variety of colors and patterns. One of the first and rarest of these is solid black. All Persians, whatever their appearance, have an extremely placid nature: they are, without doubt, the gentlest of cats.

Persian cats have been known in the West since the 17th century. One of the first Europeans to remark upon them was an Italian traveller named Pietro della Valle. He spent five years in Persia during the 1620s, and wrote the following: "There is in Persia a cat of the figure and form of ordinary ones, but infinitely more beautiful in the luster and color of its coat. It is of a blue-gray, and soft and shining as silk. The tail is of great length, and covered with hairs six inches long."

Della Valle did not just talk about this new cat, he brought some back with him to Venice and bred them. Around the same time, a French explorer brought some specimens from Turkey back to his homeland, and the Persian gradually came to be considered a highly desirable breed. By end of the 19th century it was the premier luxury cat, "the aristocrat of the cat family."Standards for the cat were established after the 1871 Crystal Palace cat show in London, UK. At that time, the list of permissible colors and patterns was limited, but the range was soon broadened to the point where one British authority, writing in 1907, could devote 127 pages of a book to the varieties of Persian.

As is often the case with popular breeds, differences have arisen between the British and American standards. Authorities in the United States favor a flatter, or more "peke-nosed," face. Moreover, in the United States, color variants are considered varieties of the same breed, while in the UK each color constitutes a separate breed. The naming convention is also different: for official purposes, Persians are known as "Longhairs" in the UK—despite the fact that there are also longhaired breeds that are not Persians.

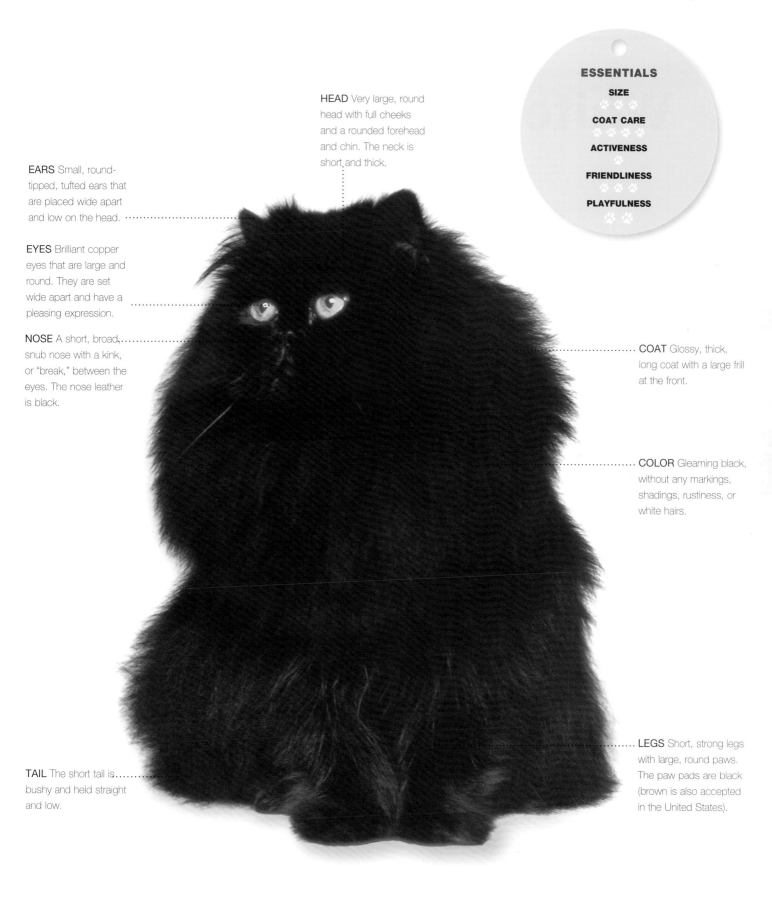

**HEAD** Very large, round head with full cheeks and a rounded forehead and chin. The neck is short and thick.

**ESSENTIALS**

SIZE

COAT CARE

ACTIVENESS

FRIENDLINESS

PLAYFULNESS

**EARS** Small, round-tipped, tufted ears that are placed wide apart and low on the head.

**EYES** Brilliant copper eyes that are large and round. They are set wide apart and have a pleasing expression.

**NOSE** A short, broad, snub nose with a kink, or "break," between the eyes. The nose leather is black.

**COAT** Glossy, thick, long coat with a large frill at the front.

**COLOR** Gleaming black, without any markings, shadings, rustiness, or white hairs.

**LEGS** Short, strong legs with large, round paws. The paw pads are black (brown is also accepted in the United States).

**TAIL** The short tail is bushy and held straight and low.

# White Persian

## WHITE PERSIAN FACTS

**PHYSIQUE** A medium-large, heavy-boned, "cobby" cat with short, sturdy legs and a broad chest, back, and shoulders. The body's rounded appearance is enhanced by the fluffy coat.

**COAT** White is one of seven recognized solid colors. The coat should be pure, dazzling white.

**TEMPERAMENT** This is a placid indoor cat with a sweet and responsive nature. The Persian enjoys play but is undemanding.

**GROOMING** The Persian's coat needs thorough daily combing to keep it tangle-free.

There is something especially glamorous about the White Persian. It is the salon cat par excellence, and is particularly popular in the United States. The White Persian was developed during the 19th-century craze for Persian cats by cross-breeding Persians with Angoras— the white variant of which has always been highly prized in its native Turkey.

The striking feature of the White Persian is undoubtedly the clean, white coat, although the eye color is also a defining quality of this beautiful cat. The two recognized colors are a stunning blue and a deep orange or copper and due to interbreeding, there is even a unique variety that has one eye of each color.

Like other Persians, the exact origins of the white variety are unknown but records indicate that white long-haired cats appeared in France over 200 years ago – this was probably when these cats began to appear in England also. Over the years these cats have been bred with other solid colors to improve the coat length and density, improving the quality of the breed overall.

In the showing environment the copper or orange eyed White Persians have been favored above the blue-eyed, as it is difficult for breeders to achieve the deep blue color that is desired for showing. Even less odd-eye White Persians have been shown, although they are still recognized and do well in competition. The white coat itself is quite a challenge to achieve, and even when pure-white kittens are born, great attention must be paid to the grooming of this variety to ensure that the coat stays clean. There are varying shades of white, from a dazzling white to a yellow-tinged white.

**ESSENTIALS**

SIZE

COAT CARE

ACTIVENESS

FRIENDLINESS

PLAYFULNESS

**HEAD** Very large, round head with full cheeks and a rounded forehead and chin. The neck is short and thick.

**EARS** Small, round-tipped, tufted ears that are placed wide apart and low on the head.

**EYES** Large, round eyes set wide apart and with a characteristically pleasing expression. The eyes may be brilliant copper, blue, or odd-eyed.

**NOSE** A short, broad, snub nose with a kink, or "break," between the eyes. The nose leather is pink.

**COLOR** The coat should be pure, dazzling white with no markings.

**COAT** Long and silky, the thick coat stands away from the body and forms a large, long frill at the front.

**LEGS** Short, strong legs with large, round paws. The paw pads are pink.

**TAIL** The short tail is bushy and held straight and low.

# Red Persian

## RED PERSIAN FACTS

🐾 **PHYSIQUE** A medium-large, heavy-boned, "cobby" cat with short, sturdy legs and a broad chest, back, and shoulders. The body's rounded appearance is enhanced by the fluffy coat.

🐾 **COAT** White is one of seven recognized solid colors. The coat should be pure, dazzling white.

🐾 **TEMPERAMENT** This is a placid indoor cat with a sweet and responsive nature. The Persian enjoys play but is undemanding.

🐾 **GROOMING** The Persian's coat needs thorough daily combing to keep it tangle-free.

Red Persians were known as "Oranges" when they arose in the 1890s. A good stock of Red Persians existed in Germany in the 1930s, but they did not survive the Second World War. They remain one of the rarer Persian breeds because it is difficult to cultivate a coat of this intense color without also promulgating obvious tabby markings.

This variety of Persians is particularly rare in the showing environment, due to the specification for completely unmarked Red Persians – a coat that is particularly difficult to breed. In the UK, slight shading on the forehead and legs is accepted (although not particularly desired), but in America the breed must have no markings whatsoever, including shading and ticking.

Although Persians originally had white undercoats, the breed should now have no white hairs and the red color should be even and bright. In young Persians, faint tabby markings may be apparent as the red coloring in the genes is not dark enough to cover the striping that is inherent in this breed's heritage. With age these may fade as the coat becomes thicker and darker. It is advisable to groom this variety often to ensure that the coat is clean and shining. Plus, the Persian's coat will shed during the summer although it will regain its thickness by winter.

A short nose is desirable for the Red Persian (as with other Persians), but the facial structure in this variety may be wider than in other Persians in general. Although these cats are usually born with blue eyes, as they mature their eyes turn an orangey, copper color.

**ESSENTIALS**

SIZE

COAT CARE

ACTIVENESS

FRIENDLINESS

PLAYFULNESS

**TAIL** The short tail is bushy and held straight and low.

**EARS** Small, round-tipped, tufted ears that are placed wide apart and low on the head.

**NOSE** A short, broad, snub nose with a kink or "break", between the eyes. The nose leather is brick red or deep pink.

**LEGS** Short, strong legs with large, round paws. The paw pads are brick red or deep pink.

**COLOR** A deep, rich red without any white hairs. Kittens often show ghost tabby markings. In the UK, slight shading on the forehead and legs in adults is acceptable, but the American standard demands no shading, ticking, or markings at all.

**HEAD** Very large, round head with full cheeks and a rounded forehead and chin. The neck is short and thick.

**EYES** Brilliant copper eyes that are large and round. They are set wide apart and have a pleasing expression.

**COAT** Glossy, thick, long coat with a large frill at the front.

# Blue Persian

## BLUE PERSIAN FACTS

**PHYSIQUE** A medium-large, heavy-boned, "cobby" cat with short, sturdy legs and a broad chest, back, and shoulders. The body's rounded appearance is enhanced by the fluffy coat.

**COAT** Blue is one of seven recognized self (solid) colors. The color is actually a pale bluish-gray.

**TEMPERAMENT** This is a placid indoor cat with a sweet and responsive nature. The Persian enjoys play but is undemanding.

**GROOMING** The Persian's coat needs thorough daily combing to keep it tangle-free.

### ESSENTIALS

**SIZE**
🐾 🐾 🐾

**COAT CARE**
🐾 🐾 🐾 🐾

**ACTIVENESS**
🐾

**FRIENDLINESS**
🐾 🐾 🐾

**PLAYFULNESS**
🐾 🐾

The Blue Persian was especially fashionable in Victorian times: Queen Victoria of England, for example, owned two "Persian Blues," as they are known. This attractive color is in fact a dilute form of black. The genetic mutation that gives rise to Persian Blues may have arisen on Malta—for this reason, cats of this color are also sometimes called Maltese Blues.

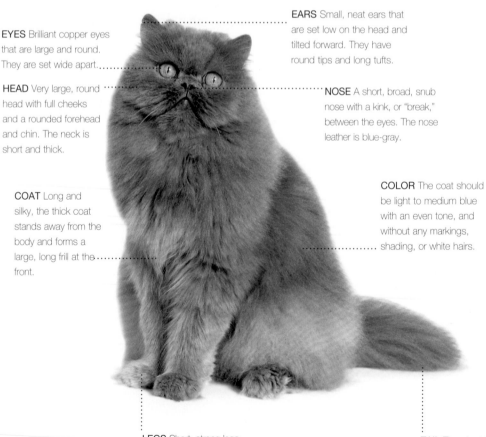

**EYES** Brilliant copper eyes that are large and round. They are set wide apart.

**HEAD** Very large, round head with full cheeks and a rounded forehead and chin. The neck is short and thick.

**COAT** Long and silky, the thick coat stands away from the body and forms a large, long frill at the front.

**EARS** Small, neat ears that are set low on the head and tilted forward. They have round tips and long tufts.

**NOSE** A short, broad, snub nose with a kink, or "break," between the eyes. The nose leather is blue-gray.

**COLOR** The coat should be light to medium blue with an even tone, and without any markings, shading, or white hairs.

**LEGS** Short, strong legs with large, round paws. The paw pads are blue-gray.

**TAIL** The short tail is bushy and held lower than the back.

# Cream Persian

The Cream Persian is one of those breeds that was at first ignored. Early British breeders called them "spoiled oranges," implying that they were no more than inferior Red Persians. But in the 1920s, the beauty of the cream Persian's richly subtle coloring came to be valued and deliberately cultivated. Modern Cream Persians are perhaps the most stylish of "dilute" Persians.

## CREAM PERSIAN FACTS

**PHYSIQUE** A medium-large, heavy-boned, "cobby" cat with short, sturdy legs and a broad chest, back, and shoulders.

**COAT** Cream is one of seven recognized self (solid) colors. The American standards call for a particular shade called "buff cream," while other authorities accept pale to medium creams.

**TEMPERAMENT** This is a placid indoor cat with a sweet and responsive nature. The Persian enjoys play but is undemanding.

**GROOMING** The Persian's coat needs thorough daily combing to keep it tangle-free.

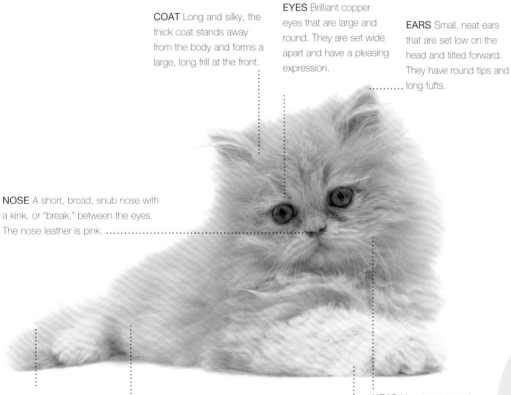

**COAT** Long and silky, the thick coat stands away from the body and forms a large, long frill at the front.

**EYES** Brilliant copper eyes that are large and round. They are set wide apart and have a pleasing expression.

**EARS** Small, neat ears that are set low on the head and tilted forward. They have round tips and long tufts.

**NOSE** A short, broad, snub nose with a kink, or "break," between the eyes. The nose leather is pink.

**TAIL** The short tail is bushy and held lower than the back.

**COLOR** The coat should be even without any markings, shading, or white hairs.

**LEGS** Short, strong legs with large, round paws. The paw pads are pink.

**HEAD** Very large, round head with full cheeks and a rounded forehead and chin. The neck is short and thick.

## ESSENTIALS

SIZE

COAT CARE

ACTIVENESS

FRIENDLINESS

PLAYFULNESS

# Chocolate Persian

## CHOCOLATE PERSIAN FACTS

**PHYSIQUE** A medium-large, heavy-boned, "cobby" cat with short, sturdy legs and a broad chest, back, and shoulders. The body's rounded appearance is enhanced by the fluffy coat.

**COAT** Chocolate is one of seven recognized solid colors. It is a rich, medium to dark chocolate color that is warm in tone.

**TEMPERAMENT** Generally a placid indoor cat with a sweet and responsive nature, the Chocolate Persian can be slightly livelier than some of the other Persians.

**GROOMING** The Persian's coat needs thorough daily combing to keep it tangle-free.

The Chocolate Persian came about as a result of the program to create Chocolate Point Persians by crossing Blue Persians and Chocolate Point Siamese. Litters containing solid-colored kittens sometimes resulted. Many of these kittens were distinctly Siamese in appearance, but careful selective breeding led to cats that were entirely Persian in appearance, yet with impeccable cocoa-colored coats.

**NOSE** A short, broad, snub nose with a kink, or "break", between the eyes. The nose leather is chocolate-brown, matching the coat.

**EYES** Brilliant copper eyes that are large and round. They are set wide apart and have a pleasing expression.

**EARS** Small, neat ears that are set low on the head and tilted forward. They have round tips and long tufts.

**COLOR** The color should be warm in tone, and even, without any markings, shading, or white hairs.

**HEAD** Very large, round head with full cheeks and a rounded forehead and chin. The neck is short and thick.

**LEGS** Short, strong legs with large, round paws. The paw pads are chocolate-brown or cinnamon-pink.

**COAT** Long and silky, the thick coat stands away from the body and forms a large, long frill at the front.

**TAIL** The short tail is bushy and held lower than the back.

## ESSENTIALS

SIZE
❀ ❀ ❀

COAT CARE
❀ ❀ ❀ ❀

ACTIVENESS
❀

FRIENDLINESS
❀ ❀ ❀

PLAYFULNESS
❀ ❀

# Lilac Persian

This one of the most delicately colored Persians. Like the Chocolate Persian, it is an offshoot of the program to produce Colorpoint Persians. The lilac coloring derives ultimately from the addition of Siamese blood to the line. This part of the Lilac Persian's genetic inheritance also has the effect of making it slightly more outgoing that other Persians.

**HEAD** Very large, round head with full cheeks and a rounded forehead and chin. The neck is short and thick.

**EARS** Small, neat ears that are set low on the head and tilted forward. They have round tips and long tufts.

**EYES** Brilliant copper eyes that are large and round. They are set wide apart and have a pleasing expression.

**NOSE** A short, broad, snub nose with a kink, or "break," between the eyes. The nose leather is lilac.

**COLOR** The color should be even pinkish-gray, warm in tone, and without any markings, shading, or white hairs.

**COAT** Long and silky, the thick coat stands away from the body and forms a large, long frill at the front.

**LEGS** Short, strong legs with large, round paws. The paw pads are lilac or pink.

**TAIL** The short tail is bushy and held lower than the back.

## LILAC PERSIAN FACTS

**PHYSIQUE** A medium-large, heavy-boned, "cobby" cat with short, sturdy legs and a broad chest, back, and shoulders. The body's rounded appearance is enhanced by the fluffy coat.

**COAT** Lilac is one of seven recognized solid colors. The color is actually a pinkish-gray.

**TEMPERAMENT** A placid indoor cat with a sweet and responsive nature, the Lilac Persian is livelier than other Persians.

**GROOMING** The Persian's coat needs thorough daily combing to keep it tangle-free.

### ESSENTIALS

SIZE

COAT CARE

ACTIVENESS

FRIENDLINESS

PLAYFULNESS

# Chinchilla Silver Persian

## CHINCHILLA SILVER PERSIAN FACTS

**PHYSIQUE** The Chinchilla has a finer bone structure than other Persians, but is still solidly built and rounded in appearance.

**COAT** Classed with the Silver Shaded and the Golden Persian. The undercoat is pure white, and the guard hairs are tipped with black to give a sparkling silver effect. In the United States, the Chinchilla Golden, which has a pale honey or apricot undercoat and black tipping, is also recognized.

**TEMPERAMENT** A placid indoor cat with a sweet and responsive nature, the Chinchilla is livelier than other Persians.

**GROOMING** The Persian's coat needs thorough daily combing to keep it tangle-free.

Known simply as the Chinchilla in the UK, the Chinchilla Silver Persian is one of the first artficially bred varieties of Persian. But successive breeding has produced a cat that is far more pure in color than the early examples. The result is a coat that shimmers like precious metal when the Chinchilla walks.

At first sight, the Chinchilla Silver Persian may be mistaken for a White Persian, as the Chinchilla's coat is predominantly translucent which makes it appear white. However, the tip of each hair contains the black pigment which gives the Chinchilla is extraordinary shimmer of silver. The 'tipping' should be evenly distributed, but the chin, ear tufts, stomach and chest should be pure white.

Another distinct quality of the Chinchilla Silver Persian is the eye color; brilliant blue-green or green that are rimmed with black, although kittens may have a blue-purple eye color that will change as the cat matures.

The Chinchilla is classed as a 'silver' cat, and attempts have been made in the US to classify this variety of Persian as a separate breed from the Persian, known as the Sterling. This was not accepted, although South African attempts to separate the breed were more successful. The Southern African Cat Council (SACC) recognizes the 'Chinchilla Longhair', which must have at least five generations in its heritage of purebred Chinchilla to be registered. This breed has a slightly longer nose than other Persians which helps the cat to breathe easier and generally improves some of the health problems that are associated with other Persians.

**ESSENTIALS**

SIZE

COAT CARE

ACTIVENESS

FRIENDLINESS

PLAYFULNESS

**EYES** Brilliant green or blue-green eyes that are rimmed with black. The large, round eyes are set wide apart and have a pleasing expression.

**EARS** Small, neat ears that are set low on the head and tilted forward. They have round tips and long tufts.

**COLOR** Snow-white fur with enough tipping on the back, flanks, head, and tail to give a silvery sheen. Chin, ear tufts, stomach, and chest are pure white with no tipping.

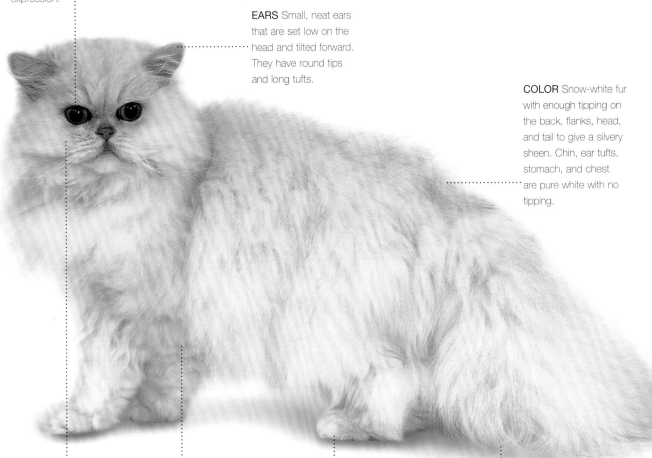

**HEAD** Very large, round head with full cheeks and a rounded forehead and chin. The mouth has a black outline.

**COAT** Long and silky, the thick coat stands away from the body and forms a large, long frill at the front.

**LEGS** Short, strong legs with large, round paws. The paw pads are black.

**TAIL** The short tail is bushy and held lower than the back.

# Shaded Silver Persian

## SHADED SILVER PERSIAN FACTS

**PHYSIQUE** A medium-large, heavy-boned, "cobby" cat with short, sturdy legs and a broad chest, back, and shoulders. The body's rounded appearance is enhanced by the fluffy coat.

**COAT** Classed with the Chinchilla and Golden Persian. The Shaded Silver is more darkly marked than the Chinchilla.

**TEMPERAMENT** A placid indoor cat with a sweet and responsive nature, the Shaded Silver Persian is livelier than other Persians.

**GROOMING** The Persian's coat needs thorough daily combing to keep it tangle-free.

Shaded Silver Persians are arrived at by crossing Chinchillas with solid colored Persians. The aim is to produce cats that have pure white undercoats with black tipping that extends for a third of the length of the hair. This is hard to achieve, but the effect can be dramatic and eye-catching.

Where the Chinchilla has a subtle silvery sheen, the intention with the Shaded Silver is to exhibit a much darker and more prevalent silver shade with more black tipping across the back, legs and tail of the cat. As with the Chinchilla, the chin, chest, stomach and inner leg should be pure white in order to achieve the best results in a showing environment. The tabby markings are undesirable in this variation. The eyes should be the brilliant green or blue green like the Chinchilla Persian, and are wide-set with a pleasant expression. It is believed that this variety was bred to improve the overall appearance and sizing of the Chinchilla.

Silver Persians are known for their domesticated temperament, and are very reliant on their owners. They tend to follow their owner from room to room which has earned them a 'dog-like' reputation, they are affectionate and loving, and may choose a 'special' person in the family as the favorite. The Shaded Silver Persian is said to be livelier than other Persians, and is a very responsive variety.

As with other long-haired cats, the Shaded Silver requires regular grooming to prevent matting and to keep the coat in fine condition – a daily combing is recommended. A sweet, indoor cat with an inquisitive nature.

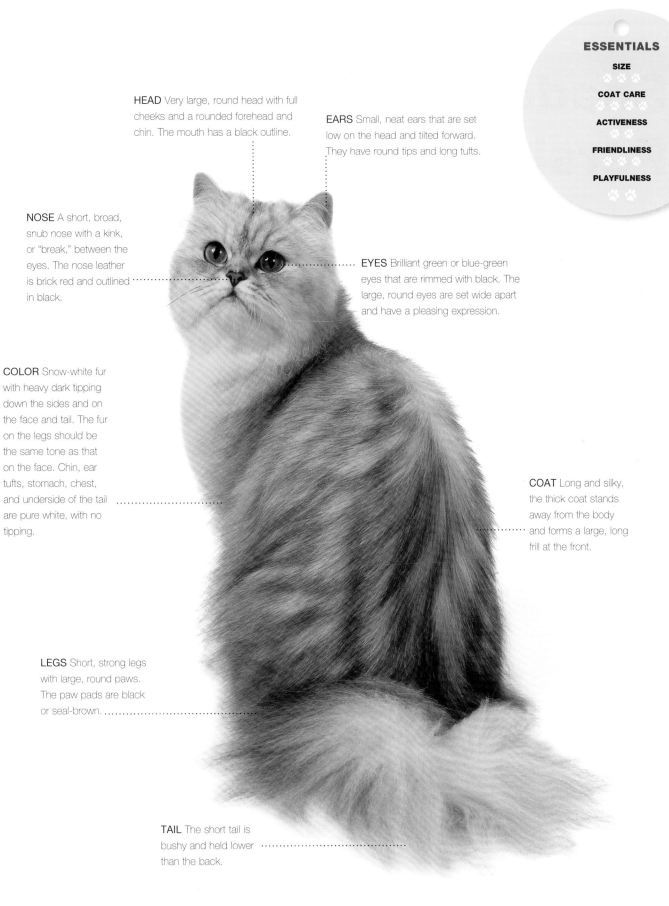

**HEAD** Very large, round head with full cheeks and a rounded forehead and chin. The mouth has a black outline.

**EARS** Small, neat ears that are set low on the head and tilted forward. They have round tips and long tufts.

**NOSE** A short, broad, snub nose with a kink, or "break," between the eyes. The nose leather is brick red and outlined in black.

**EYES** Brilliant green or blue-green eyes that are rimmed with black. The large, round eyes are set wide apart and have a pleasing expression.

**COLOR** Snow-white fur with heavy dark tipping down the sides and on the face and tail. The fur on the legs should be the same tone as that on the face. Chin, ear tufts, stomach, chest, and underside of the tail are pure white, with no tipping.

**COAT** Long and silky, the thick coat stands away from the body and forms a large, long frill at the front.

**LEGS** Short, strong legs with large, round paws. The paw pads are black or seal-brown.

**TAIL** The short tail is bushy and held lower than the back.

**ESSENTIALS**

**SIZE**

**COAT CARE**

**ACTIVENESS**

**FRIENDLINESS**

**PLAYFULNESS**

# Shaded Golden Persian

## SHADED GOLDEN PERSIAN FACTS

**PHYSIQUE** The Shaded Golden has a finer bone structure than other Persians, but is still solidly built and rounded in appearance. It has the Persian's characteristically stocky legs and bushy tail.

**COAT** Classed with the Chinchilla and Shaded Silver. The Shaded Golden has a apricot to gold undercoat with dark tipping down the sides, face, and tail.

**TEMPERAMENT** A placid indoor cat with a sweet and responsive nature, the Shaded Golden is livelier than other Persians.

**GROOMING** The Persian's coat needs thorough daily combing to keep it tangle-free.

Known simply as Golden Persians in the UK, Shaded Goldens sometimes appeared unexpectedly in litters of Shaded Silver Persians. The golden effect derives from seal-brown or black tipping on an apricot base—which makes these cats look like an even more precious version of their silvery cousins. Shaded Goldens were recognized as a separate breed in the 1980s.

**EYES** Brilliant green or blue-green eyes that are rimmed with black. The large, round eyes are set wide apart and have a pleasing expression.

**EARS** Small, neat ears that are set low on the head and tilted forward. They have round tips and long tufts.

**COAT** Long and silky, the thick coat stands away from the body and forms a large, long frill at the front.

**COLOR** The tipping brings a golden appearance to the sides and on the face and tail. The chin, ear tufts, stomach, chest, and underside of the tail are pale gold with no tipping.

**ESSENTIALS**

**SIZE**

**COAT CARE**

**ACTIVENESS**

**FRIENDLINESS**

**PLAYFULNESS**

**HEAD** Very large, round head with full cheeks and a rounded forehead and chin. The mouth has a black outline.

**NOSE** A short, broad, snub nose with a kink, or "break," between the eyes. The nose leather is rose-colored or brick red, and outlined in black.

**LEGS** Short, strong legs with large, round paws. The paw pads are black or seal-brown.

**TAIL** The short tail is bushy and held lower than the back.

# Cameo Persian

Cameo Persians have pure white undercoats with guard hairs tipped in a different color. This creates a shimmering effect that is identical to the dazzling coat of the Chinchilla—except that in the case of the Cameo, the color of the tipping can vary. Cameo Persians come in varieties as diverse as red, cream, tortoiseshell, and blue-cream.

**HEAD** Very large, round head with full cheeks and a rounded forehead and chin. The neck is short and thick.

**EYES** Brilliant copper eyes that are large and round. They are set wide apart and have a pleasing expression.

**COLOR** The Shell Cameo has a white undercoat and tipping restricted to the ends of the guard hairs; the Shaded Cameo has heavier tipping, forming a mantle effect down the sides, face, and tail.

**EARS** Small, round-tipped, tufted ears that are placed wide apart and low on the head.

**NOSE** A short, broad, snub nose with a kink, or "break," between the eyes. The nose leather complements the color of the tipping.

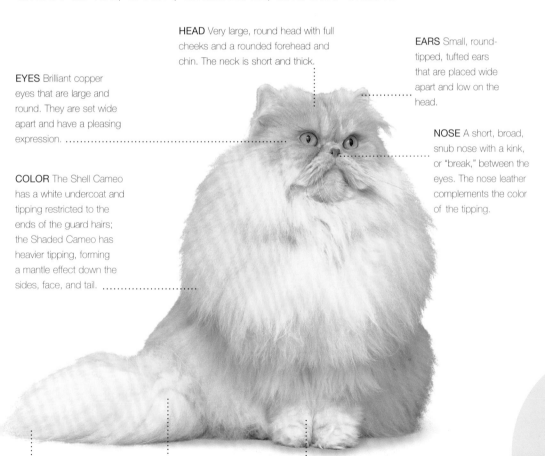

**TAIL** The short tail is bushy and held lower than the back.

**COAT** Glossy, thick, long coat with a large frill at the front.

**LEGS** Short, strong legs with large, round paws. The paw pads complement the color of the tipping.

## CAMEO PERSIAN FACTS

**PHYSIQUE** A medium-large, heavy-boned, "cobby" cat.

**COAT** The Cameo is classed under Smoked and Shaded cats in the United States, but is treated separately in the UK. There are two types: the Shell Cameo and the Shaded Cameo. Red, cream, tortoiseshell, and blue-cream varieties are accepted in the United States, with a wider range recognized elsewhere.

**TEMPERAMENT** This is a placid indoor cat with a sweet and responsive nature. The Persian enjoys play but is undemanding.

**GROOMING** The Persian's coat needs thorough daily combing to keep it tangle-free.

### ESSENTIALS

SIZE

COAT CARE

ACTIVENESS

FRIENDLINESS

PLAYFULNESS

# Pewter Persian

## PEWTER PERSIAN FACTS

🐾 **PHYSIQUE** A medium-large, heavy-boned, "cobby" cat with short, sturdy legs and a broad chest, back, and shoulders. The body's rounded appearance is enhanced by the fluffy coat.

🐾 **COAT** Both Black and Blue Pewter Persians are recognized in the UK. The undercoat is pure white, with black or blue tipping to the guard hairs.

🐾 **TEMPERAMENT** Companionable and sweet-natured, but can be livelier than other Persians.

🐾 **GROOMING** The Persian's coat needs thorough daily combing to keep it tangle-free.

The Pewter Persian is sometimes confused with the Shaded Silver Persian. Their tipped coats look very alike, but the Pewter Persian is easily told apart by its copper or orange eyes (Shaded Silver Persians always have emerald or blue eyes). The Pewter Persian is currently not recognized outside of the UK.

**HEAD** Very large, round head with full cheeks and a rounded forehead and chin. The mouth has a black outline.

**EARS** Small, neat ears that are set low on the head and tilted forward. They have round tips and long tufts.

**EYES** Brilliant copper eyes that are rimmed with black. The large, round eyes are set wide apart and have a pleasing expression.

**NOSE** A short, broad, snub nose with a kink, or "break", between the eyes. The nose leather complements the color of the coat and has a dark outline.

**COLOR** White fur with dark tipping for a shaded effect over the head, back, flanks, and legs. The chin, stomach, chest, and underside of the tail should be silvery white.

**LEGS** Short, strong legs with large, round paws. The paw pads complement the color of the coat.

**TAIL** The short tail is bushy and held lower than the back.

**COAT** Long and silky, the thick coat stands away from the body and forms a large, long frill at the front.

### ESSENTIALS

**SIZE**
🐾 🐾 🐾

**COAT CARE**
🐾 🐾 🐾 🐾 🐾

**ACTIVENESS**
🐾 🐾 🐾

**FRIENDLINESS**
🐾 🐾 🐾 🐾

**PLAYFULNESS**
🐾 🐾

# Smoke Persian

The Smoke Persian is mentioned in records as far back as the 1860s, but became rare in the first half of the 20th century. Its coat is so deeply tipped that the white undercoat may only become apparent when the cat moves. The luxuriant frill and ear tufts are silvery white, making a striking contast with the rest of the coat.

## SMOKE PERSIAN FACTS

**PHYSIQUE** A medium-large, heavy-boned, "cobby" cat.

**COAT** Smoke Persians are classed on their own in the UK and in the Smoke and Shaded class in the United States. The traditional smoke colors are black and blue, but other colors, including blue-cream, and tortoiseshell, are now accepted.

**TEMPERAMENT** This is a placid indoor cat with a sweet and responsive nature. The Persian enjoys play but is undemanding.

**GROOMING** The Persian's coat needs thorough daily combing to keep it tangle-free.

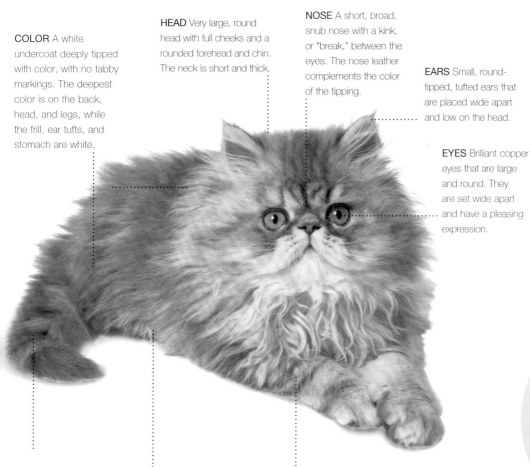

**COLOR** A white undercoat deeply tipped with color, with no tabby markings. The deepest color is on the back, head, and legs, while the frill, ear tufts, and stomach are white.

**HEAD** Very large, round head with full cheeks and a rounded forehead and chin. The neck is short and thick.

**NOSE** A short, broad, snub nose with a kink, or "break," between the eyes. The nose leather complements the color of the tipping.

**EARS** Small, round-tipped, tufted ears that are placed wide apart and low on the head.

**EYES** Brilliant copper eyes that are large and round. They are set wide apart and have a pleasing expression.

**TAIL** The short tail is bushy and held straight and low.

**COAT** Glossy, thick, long coat with a large frill at the front.

**LEGS** Short, strong legs with large, round paws. The paw pads harmonize with the color of the tipping.

### ESSENTIALS

**SIZE**
🐾🐾🐾

**COAT CARE**
🐾🐾🐾🐾

**ACTIVENESS**
🐾

**FRIENDLINESS**
🐾🐾🐾

**PLAYFULNESS**
🐾🐾

# Tabby Persian

## TABBY PERSIAN FACTS

**PHYSIQUE** A medium-large, heavy-boned, "cobby" cat.

**COAT** Only the classic tabby pattern is recognized in the UK, but mackerel, spotted, and ticked tabby patterns are accepted elsewhere. The traditional colors are brown, silver, and red, but other varieties, including cream and cameo, are also recognized.

**TEMPERAMENT** Tabby Persians can be more independent than other varieties, but have the same sweet disposition.

**GROOMING** Thorough daily combing needed; care must be taken to bring out the coat pattern.

The Tabby Persian has been known for 200 years, but the modern version emerged at the end of the 19th century. It is much rarer than the shorthaired version of the Tabby. This is probably due in part to the fact that the classic tabby pattern is much harder to show to advantage in a long coat.

**EARS** Small, neat ears that are set low on the head and tilted forward. They have round tips and long tufts.

**EYES** Brilliant eyes that are large and round. They are set wide apart and have a pleasing expression. Most Tabby Persians have copper eyes, but Silver varieties may have green, hazel, or copper eyes.

**HEAD** Very large, round head with full cheeks and a rounded forehead and chin. The neck is short and thick.

**NOSE** A short, broad, snub nose with a kink, or "break", between the eyes. The nose leather harmonizes with the c[o] color.

**TAIL** The short tail is bushy and held lower than the back.

**COAT** Long and silky, the thick coat stands away from the body and forms a large, long frill at the front.

**COLOR** The classic tabby has an "M" on the forehead, a butterfly-shaped shoulder marking, three stripes down the back, and a spiral ("oyster") on each flank.

**LEGS** Short, strong leg[s] with large, round paws. The paw pads should complement the tabby coat color.

## ESSENTIALS

**SIZE**

**COAT CARE**

**ACTIVENESS**

**FRIENDLINESS**

**PLAYFULNESS**

# Tortoiseshell Persian

Opinions vary as to the ideal look for a Tortie Persian. In the United States, the preferred tortoiseshell pattern consists of distinct bands or patches of color. In the UK, the most desirable coats have colors that are mingled and mixed. All authorities look for a dashing blaze of red or cream on the forehead.

**EARS** Small, round-tipped, tufted ears that are placed wide apart and low on the head.

**EYES** Brilliant copper eyes that are large and round. They are set wide apart and have a pleasing expression.

**HEAD** Very large, round head with full cheeks and a rounded forehead and chin. The neck is short and thick.

**NOSE** A short, broad, snub nose with a kink, or "break," between the eyes. The nose leather color complements the coat.

**COLOR** The colors on a Tortie's coat may be softly intermingled (as required in the UK) or form distinct patches (as preferred in the United States).

**COAT** Glossy, thick, long coat with a large frill at the front.

**LEGS** Short, strong legs with large, round paws. The paw pads harmonize with the coat color.

**TAIL** The short tail is bushy and held straight and low.

## TORTOISESHELL PERSIAN FACTS

**PHYSIQUE** A medium-large, heavy-boned, "cobby" cat with short, sturdy legs and a broad chest, back, and shoulders. The body's rounded appearance is enhanced by the fluffy coat.

**COAT** The traditional tortie coloring is black with patches of red. The Chocolate Tortie, Blue-Cream, and Lilac-Cream are dilute variations.

**TEMPERAMENT** This is a placid indoor cat with a sweet and responsive nature. The Persian enjoys play but is undemanding.

**GROOMING** Thorough daily combing needed; care must be taken to bring out the coat pattern.

### ESSENTIALS

**SIZE**
🐾🐾🐾

**COAT CARE**
🐾🐾🐾🐾

**ACTIVENESS**
🐾

**FRIENDLINESS**
🐾🐾🐾

**PLAYFULNESS**
🐾🐾

# Blue-Cream Persian

## BLUE-CREAM PERSIAN FACTS

**PHYSIQUE** A medium-large, heavy-boned, "cobby" cat with short, sturdy legs and a broad chest, back, and shoulders. The body's rounded appearance is enhanced by the fluffy coat.

**COAT** The Blue-Cream is a dilute version of the Tortoiseshell with blue and cream replacing the standard black and red coloring.

**TEMPERAMENT** This is a placid indoor cat with a sweet and responsive nature. The Persian enjoys play but is undemanding.

**GROOMING** The Persian's coat needs thorough daily combing to keep it tangle-free.

Blue-Cream Persians have been produced since the early days of the Persian breed. At first they were created by accident and then used in breeding programs for Creams and Blues. But they came to be prized for their beautiful mottled coat, which has been described as having the appearance of shot silk. The Blue-Cream Persian was formally recognized in 1930.

**COLOR** The coat should comprise pastel blue and cream. The UK standard requires the colors to be softly intermingled to the extremities, but the United States also accepts distinct patches of color.

**EARS** Small, neat ears that are set low on the head and tilted forward. They have round tips and long tufts.

**EYES** Brilliant copper eyes that are large and round. They are set wide apart and have a pleasing expression.

**COAT** Long and silky, the thick coat stands away from the body and forms a large, long frill at the front.

## ESSENTIALS

**SIZE**

**COAT CARE**

**ACTIVENESS**

**FRIENDLINESS**

**PLAYFULNESS**

**TAIL** The short tail is bushy and held lower than the back.

**LEGS** Short, strong legs with large, round paws. The paw pads are blue or pink.

**NOSE** A short, broad, snub nose with a kink, or "break," between the eyes. The nose leather is blue or pink.

**HEAD** Very large, round head with full cheeks and a rounded forehead and chin. The neck is short and thick.

# Bicolor Persian

Bicolor Persians were once frowned upon by serious breeders: they looked too much like common street cats. But they came to be accepted, and definite standards were introduced. A stipulation that the white patches be symmetrical was dropped because it was too difficult to achieve—but a clear, inverted "V" on the nose is still preferred.

## BICOLOR PERSIAN FACTS

**PHYSIQUE** A medium-large, heavy-boned, "cobby" cat with short, sturdy legs and a broad chest, back, and shoulders.

**COAT** White plus another solid color: black, blue, red, cream, chocolate, or lilac. Other accepted varieties include tabby and white, cameo and white, and calico (tortie and white).

**TEMPERAMENT** This is a placid indoor cat with a sweet and responsive nature. The Persian enjoys play but is undemanding.

**GROOMING** The Persian's coat needs thorough daily combing to keep it tangle-free.

**EYES** Brilliant eyes that are large and round. They are set wide apart and have a pleasing expression. The UK standard calls for copper eyes, while the United States accepts copper, blue, or odd-eye color.

**HEAD** Very large, round head with full cheeks, rounded forehead and chin, carried on a short and thick neck. The short, broad, snub nose has a "break," or kink, between the eyes, and a nose leather that complements the main coat color.

**EARS** Small, round-tipped, tufted ears that are placed wide apart and low on the head.

**COAT** Glossy, thick, long coat with a large frill at the front.

**COLOR** The patches of color should be even, with no white hairs, and the white parts should be pure white with no markings. The undersides, muzzle, chest, legs, and feet should be white (the UK accepts some color here).

**LEGS** Short, strong legs with large, round paws. The paw pads harmonize with the main color.

**TAIL** The short tail is bushy and held straight and low.

### ESSENTIALS

SIZE

COAT CARE

ACTIVENESS

FRIENDLINESS

PLAYFULNESS

# Calico Persian

The Calico Persian is so-called in the United States because its coat resembles the popular printed cotton. In the UK the pattern was once called "Chintz," but is now known rather long-windedly as tortoiseshell-and-white. As with Bicolors, the American standard calls for well-defined patches of color, mostly on the underparts. In the UK, any degree of white is acceptable.

The Calico cat is a very popular tri-color type of cat and although it can be found among several different breeds, the Persian is a unique and striking variety of calico cat that is found is several color combinations. The color of the calico depends on the genetics of the mother and father; in Persians you can find tortoiseshell-white varieties and also blue-cream calico varieties, plus chocolate and lilac varieties.

The most desirable calico Persian for showing would have a combination of black, red and white tortoiseshell. There is a minimum degree of white that a calico must show, usually on the under-parts and legs, although the UK is more lenient with the amount of white on the cat. It is acceptable for the eye color to differ, although blue, hazel and copper are desirable.

If the cat has different color eyes, this is acceptable also.

The Calico Persian is sometimes described as 'uncommon' because breeders don't often aim for this coloring, although it is not rare and can be found quite easily. It is a beautiful cat and like all Persians, needs regular brushing to keep the extraordinary coat in good condition. This cat is dignified, independent and quiet although they do love human companionship. It is not ideal to leave this breed alone for long periods of time, as they do like affection from their owner.

**ESSENTIALS**

SIZE

COAT CARE

ACTIVENESS

FRIENDLINESS

PLAYFULNESS

**HEAD** Very large, round head with full cheeks and a rounded forehead and chin. The neck is short and thick.

**EARS** Small, round-tipped, tufted ears that are placed wide apart and low on the head.

**EYES** Brilliant eyes that are large, round, and set wide apart. The UK standard specifies copper eyes, but the United States accepts a wider range of eye color.

**COAT** Glossy, thick, long coat with a large frill at the front.

**NOSE** A short, broad, snub nose with a kink, or "break," between the eyes. The nose leather complements the coat.

**COLOR** The patches of color should be even, with no white hairs, and the white parts should be pure white with no markings. The undersides, muzzle, chest, legs, and the feet should be white (the UK accepts some color here).

**LEGS** Short, strong legs with large, round paws. The paw pads harmonize with the main color.

**TAIL** The short tail is bushy and held straight and low.

# Himalayan

## HIMALAYAN FACTS

**PHYSIQUE** A medium-large, heavy-boned, "cobby" cat with short, sturdy legs and a broad chest, back, and shoulders. The body's rounded appearance is enhanced by the fluffy coat.

**COAT** The solid point colors are seal, blue, chocolate, lilac, flame (red), and cream. Tortoiseshell, lynx/tabby, and tortie lynx/tabby points are also recognized.

**TEMPERAMENT** A placid indoor cat with a sweet and responsive nature. The Himalayan (Colorpoint) Persian tends to be more spirited than other varieties.

**GROOMING** The Persian's coat needs thorough daily combing to keep it tangle-free.

Himalayans, known as Colorpoints in the UK, are Persians with Siamese markings. The first attempts to impose the pointed coloring of the Siamese on the Persian type were made in the 1920s. But it was not until the 1950s that the Himalayan first made its show debut. A wide range of point colors has since been developed.

There has been much debate over whether the Himalayan is simply another color strand of the Persian, or whether it should be categorized as a different breed due to its different ancestry. The International Cat Association classes the Himalayan as a separate breed; however it is grouped together with the Persian and the Exotic Shorthair (a short-haired Persian) in the Persian Breed Group standard. The Cat Fanciers Association however, classes the cat as a colour variation of the Persian, which competes in its own color category.

Unlike the Persian, whose round 'cobby' body sometimes prevents it from jumping particularly high, the Himalayan's Siamese ancestry means that it has less of the jumping limitations than the Persian, as it has taken on the body shape of the Siamese. However, just because they can, doesn't mean they do! The Himalayan likes to lounge about rather than jump or climb, although their Siamese heritage makes them more active than other strains of Persian. They do enjoy playing, in a calm manner.

The Himalayan has striking blue eyes, inherited from the Siamese. This is one of the defining features of a Himalayan – affectionately known as the 'Himmy' – and one that makes this one of the most popular Persians around. This breed has also been popularized by the media, making many appearances in television and film.

**HEAD** Very large, round head with full cheeks and a rounded forehead and chin. The neck is short and thick.

**EARS** Small, round-tipped, tufted ears that are placed wide apart and low on the head.

**EYES** Brilliant sapphire blue eyes that are large and round. They are set wide apart and have a pleasing expression.

**NOSE** A short, broad, snub nose with a kink, or "break," between the eyes. The nose leather harmonizes with the coat's point color.

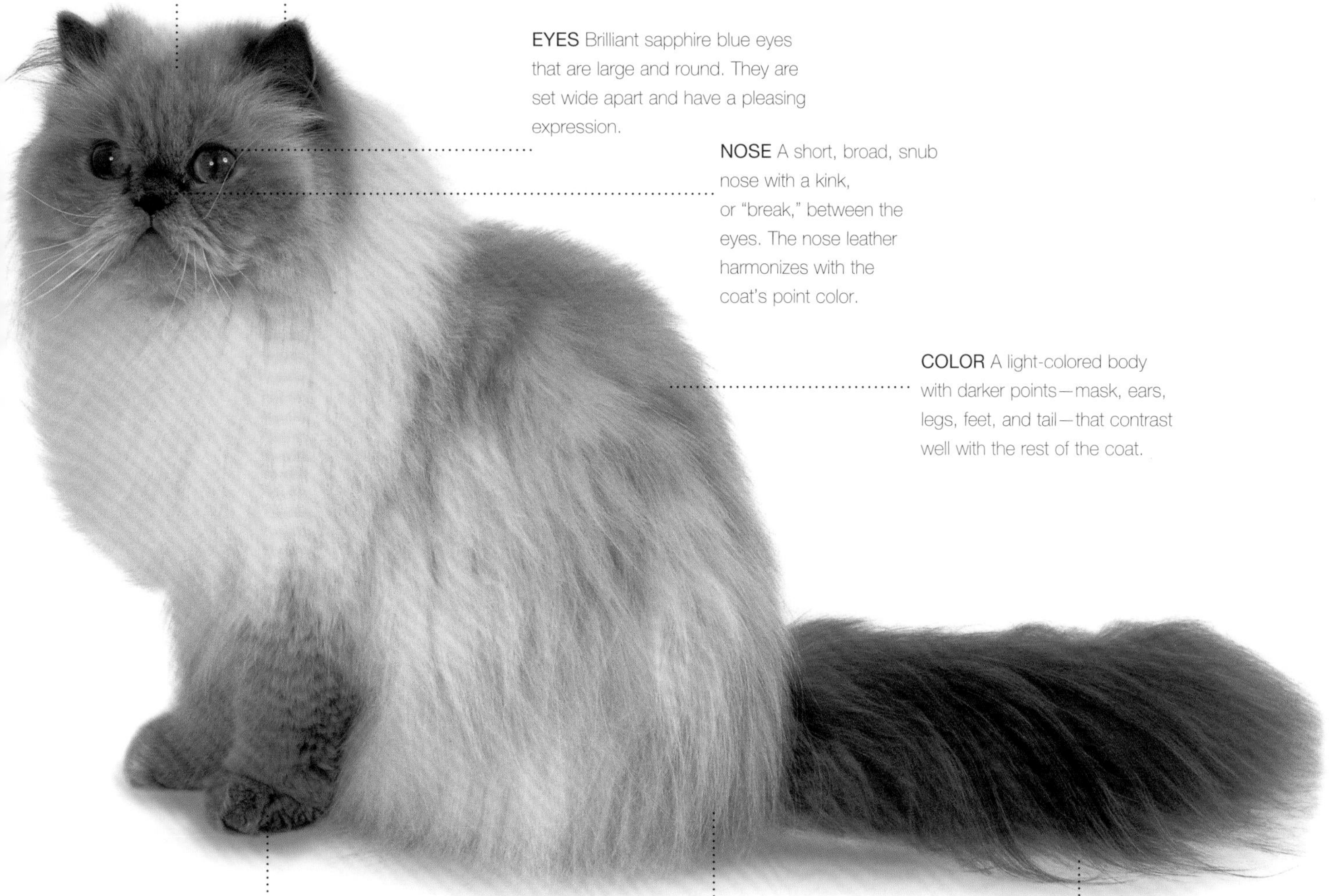

**COLOR** A light-colored body with darker points—mask, ears, legs, feet, and tail—that contrast well with the rest of the coat.

**LEGS** Short, strong legs with large, round paws. The paw pads harmonize with the point color.

**COAT** Glossy, thick, long coat with a large frill at the front.

**TAIL** The short tail is bushy and held straight and low.

**ESSENTIALS**

SIZE

COAT CARE

ACTIVENESS

FRIENDLINESS

PLAYFULNESS

# Other Longhaired Cats

Longhaired cats are much less common than shorthaired. Some have developed as natural breeds in cold countries such as Russia, some are the result of a genetic mutation that has been carefully cultivated, and others have been deliberately bred as longhaired variants of an established shorthaired breed. In general, these cats have fur that is less woolly and less full than that of a Persian, so they are easier to groom. However, almost all longhaired cats still need regular brushing, and they all have a tendency to molt.

# Maine Coon

## MAINE COON FACTS

**PHYSIQUE** A large, muscular, and broad-chested cat. The breed is slow to mature, but fully grown males can weigh 20 lb (9 kg).

**COAT** The Maine Coon is recognized in most colors and patterns.

**TEMPERAMENT** An active but companiable cat, the Maine Coon is easy to train and enjoys playing games.

**GROOMING** The coat is virtually self-maintaining, but regular combing and brushing will keep it looking its best.

The Maine Coon is one of the largest domestic cats, and it is the oldest American breed. It has always been a working cat: in the early days it earned its keep as a ratter on the farms of New England. It is also one of the best tree climbers in the cat kingdom.

The Maine Coon has been known by many names, among them the American Shag, the American Forest Cat, and the Maine Trick Cat. Its present name derives from the fact that its bushy tail and tree-climbing skills lend it a passing resemblance (at a distance, at least) to a raccoon. It was once even supposed that the Maine Coon was a cross between a cat and a raccoon—which is, of course, zoological nonsense.

Some of the theories as to how the Maine Coon arrived in America are barely less fanciful. Its resemblance to the Norwegian Forest Cat spawned the idea that the Maine Coon was introduced by the Vikings a thousand years ago, despite scant evidence that the Vikings reached the North American mainland. A more romantic story claims that the Maine Coon is descended on one side from six Angoras that were the treasured possessions of Marie Antoinette. She had them sent to America, hoping to join them once she escaped the clutches of the revolutionaries. She never made it, but her cats got to America, where they interbred with local tabbies. Certainly such a cross might result in a cat that looked something like the Maine Coon, but that is all the legend has to recommend it.

By far the most likely explanation is that the Maine Coon is descended from domestic cats that turned feral, then developed a large bulk and a thick coat as protection against the harsh winters of New England. One thing known for certain about the Maine Coon is that it was the first cat to be exhibited in shows.Cats competed for the title of State Champion Coon Cat at annual fairs in Maine a decade before the first London cat show of 1871.

**ESSENTIALS**

SIZE

COAT CARE

ACTIVENESS

FRIENDLINESS

PLAYFULNESS

**HEAD** A long head with a squarish muzzle, and a chin that is in alignment with the nose. The nose leather complements the color of the coat.

**EARS** Large ears that are wide at the base and taper to a rounded, feathered point.

**COAT** A heavy, shaggy, double coat with longer hair forming a distinct ruff at the front, and britches on the back legs. The coat is silky to the touch, and water-resistant. Some coat is lost during summer.

**EYES** Widely spaced, large, expressive eyes that are slightly slanted. They are usually copper, green, gold, or green-gold. White or bicolor cats may have blue or odd-colored eyes.

**LEGS** Strong, straight legs of medium length. The paws are large and round, with tufts between the toes, and pads that complement the color of the coat.

**TAIL** Long, plume-like tail that is wide at the base and tapering. It is carried high off the ground.

# Balinese

## BALINESE FACTS

🐾 **PHYSIQUE** The Balinese has a long, fine-boned, lithe body with a slender neck and long, slim legs.

🐾 **COAT** In the United States, only the seal point, chocolate point, blue point, and lilac point versions are recognized. Other associations accept non-traditional colors such as red and cream, as well as tortie and tabby varieties.

🐾 **TEMPERAMENT** A highly inquisitive, energetic, and playful cat. Ideally the Balinese needs feline as well as human company.

🐾 **GROOMING** Daily brushing and combing is advisable.

The Balinese is, in essence, a longhaired Siamese. "Longhaired Siamese" was, in fact, the name by which these cats were known for a time after the breed first appeared. But breeders of classic Siamese cats objected to this extension of use of the Siamese name, and a new designation was adopted for these elegant, longhaired cats.

The Balinese cat does not actually hail from the Indonesian island of Bali. But Bali is close to Siam (Thailand) and so the name is a poetic way of acknowledging the genetic relationship of the Balinese to the Siamese cat. The name is also an indication of the Balinese cat's physical presence, which is reminiscent of the graceful posturing of an Indonesian temple dancer. In the 1930s and 1940s, there were attempts to produce longhaired Siamese by crossing them with Angoras. But these experiments nearly always resulted in shorthaired offspring. At the same time, pedigree Siamese occasionally produced longhaired kittens—one was registered in Britain as early as 1928. It is not clear whether these oddities were the result of spontaneous mutation, or of outcrossing somewhere in the parents' ancestry. But whatever their provenance, the longhaired rarities were generally seen as worthless from a breeding point of view.

That changed in the 1950s, when a Californian breeder named Marion Dorset took an interest in this occasional cat, and developed a breeding program designed to promulgate it. Balinese were first exhibited in the United States in 1955, and were recognized by most associations during the 1960s. Repeated back-crossing with purebred Siamese has produced Balinese with a shorter and less evident coat: some are distinguished from Siamese by no more than a furry underbelly and a slightly bushier tail. However, some breeders are now promoting a Traditional Balinese, with a sturdier body and more rounded muzzle and ears. In the 1970s the Balinese was exported to Europe, where breeders developed variants other than the four classic Siamese colors (seal point, chocolate point, blue point, and lilac point). In the United States, these newer Balinese types are known as Javanese—an extension of the geographical idea that inspired the original name.

**ESSENTIALS**

SIZE

COAT CARE

ACTIVENESS

FRIENDLINESS

PLAYFULNESS

**COLOR** A pale body that is lighter on the underparts. There is a distinct contrast with the darker coloring on the face, ears, legs, and tail.

**EARS** Very large ears that are wide at the base and taper into points. They form a triangle with the pointed chin.

**COAT** Medium-length, fine, and silky coat.

**EYES** Almond-shaped, slanted eyes that are brilliant blue in color.

**HEAD** Elongated, wedge-shaped head, with a straight profile and well-defined chin.

**TAIL** Long, flowing tail that tapers to a slender tip.

**LEGS** The legs are long and slender, and the hind legs are longer than the forelegs.

**PAWS** Dainty little oval paws with pads that complement the color of the points.

# Turkish Angora

## TURKISH ANGORA FACTS

**PHYSIQUE** Small to medium cat, with a long, slender body that is well-muscled.

**COAT** The Turkish Angora is recognized in Western self (solid) and tortie colors, in solid, smoke, shaded, bicolor, tabby (classic, mackerel, spotted, patched), and silver tabby patterns.

**TEMPERAMENT** One of the most outgoing of cat breeds, the Turkish Angora is assertive, playful, and very lively.

**GROOMING** Regular combing will keep the coat in top condition.

The Turkish Angora is the national cat of Turkey, where it has been known for centuries: the very name Angora is the old form of Ankara, Turkey's capital city. The cat comes in a wide range of colors and patterns, but in its native land a pure white coat (coupled with odd-colored eyes) is prized above all.

Legend has it that the Turkish Angora evolved from the central Asian wild cat known as the manul, which was tamed by the horsemen of Genghis Khan and came to Turkey with them. A far more likely scenario is that the long hair of the Turkish Angora came about as a result of a chance genetic mutation.

Turkish Angoras, along with Persians, found their way to western Europe in the 17th and 18th centuries. From the start, the two breeds were often confused and conflated and, for a while, all longhaired cats were indiscriminately called Angoras. When the Persian cat became overwhelmingly popular in the 19th century, the fortunes of Turkish Angoras plummeted. They were so widely used in breeding to improve the Persian coat that they became practically subsumed in the Persian line—and came very close to disappearing altogether.

It is claimed (although the story may be almost as mythical as the link with Genghis Khan) that the Turkish Angora was saved by events in its native land. At the end of the First World War, in the first patriotic rush of enthusiasm for the new Turkish republic, a breeding program was initiated at Ankara Zoo to ensure the survival of the national cat. If that is truly how the Turkish Angora was preserved, then the project was a great success. Angoras were plentiful by the 1960s, when western breeders rediscovered the cat and began breeding programs of their own.

Despite its documented history, the Turkish Angora is not recognized in the UK. During the Turkish Angora's long absence from the international scene, an entirely separate breed of longhaired cats, bred in the UK from an Abyssinian and a Seal Point Siamese, borrowed the Angora name (see p.104).

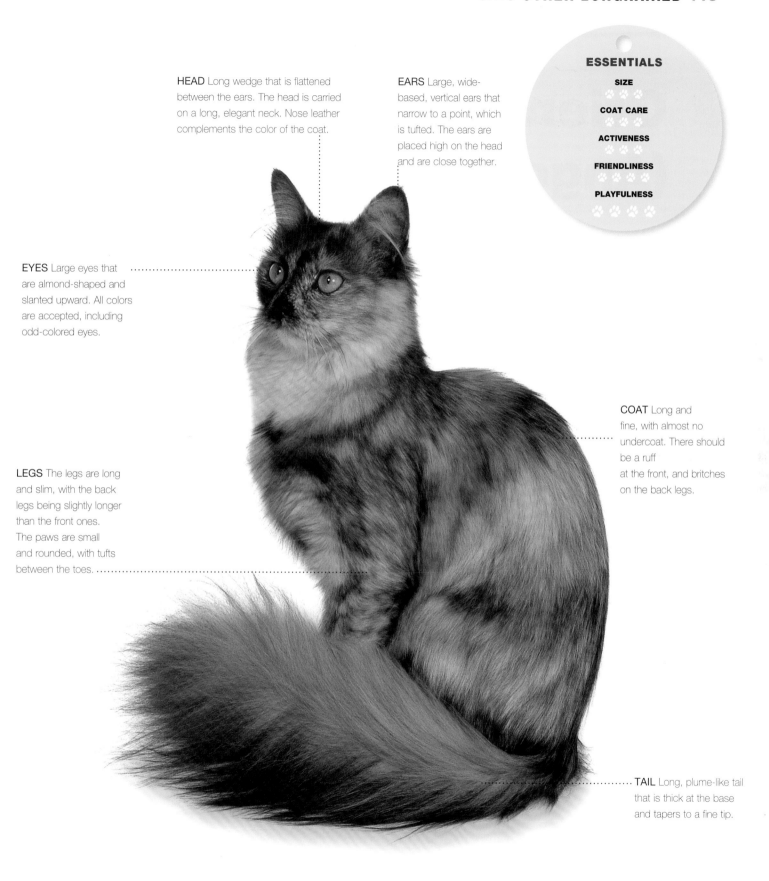

**HEAD** Long wedge that is flattened between the ears. The head is carried on a long, elegant neck. Nose leather complements the color of the coat.

**EARS** Large, wide-based, vertical ears that narrow to a point, which is tufted. The ears are placed high on the head and are close together.

**ESSENTIALS**

SIZE

COAT CARE

ACTIVENESS

FRIENDLINESS

PLAYFULNESS

**EYES** Large eyes that are almond-shaped and slanted upward. All colors are accepted, including odd-colored eyes.

**COAT** Long and fine, with almost no undercoat. There should be a ruff at the front, and britches on the back legs.

**LEGS** The legs are long and slim, with the back legs being slightly longer than the front ones. The paws are small and rounded, with tufts between the toes.

**TAIL** Long, plume-like tail that is thick at the base and tapers to a fine tip.

# Oriental Longhair (Angora)

## ORIENTAL LONGHAIR (ANGORA) FACTS

🐾 **PHYSIQUE** A medium-sized cat with a long, svelte body that is well-muscled.

🐾 **COAT** The Oriental Longhair (Angora) comes in all self (solid) and tortie colors. There are also solid, smoke, shaded, tabby, and silver tabby varieties.

🐾 **TEMPERAMENT** This playful, sociable cat enjoys human and feline company. It can be vocal.

🐾 **GROOMING** Regular combing is recommended to keep the coat well maintained.

The Oriental Longhair (Angora) was developed in Britain in the middle of the 20th century. During this time, the true Turkish Angora seemed to have disappeared completely, and the aim was to recreate the sumptuous longhaired cat known from 19th-century paintings. The cumbersome bracketed name was adopted after the Turkish Angora re-established itself on the international scene.

The breed officially designated the Oriental Longhair (Angora) in the UK is known by a bewildering variety of names elsewhere. In France and other countries of mainland Europe, it is generally known as the Javanese in order to avoid confusion with the Turkish Angora, to which it is not related. Some registries prefer to call it the Mandarin. In the United States and Canada, where the word Javanese is used as a blanket term for certain shades of the Balinese, the Oriental Longhair (Angora) is not known. To complete the mystifying picture, there is a quite separate breed also called the Oriental Longhair (see p.106), which has been developed from the Oriental Shorthair. However, this particular breed of many pseudonyms originated in the late 1960s, when a litter was born as a result of a mating between a sorrel Abyssinian and a Seal Point Siamese. Their owner, a breeder named Maureen Silson, used them as the basis of a breeding program and within a few generations she had produced a longhaired cat of the oriental type that had the cinnamon gene of its Abyssinian forebear. Silson described it as a "longhaired Havana"; today, it would be termed a cinnamon Oriental Longhair (Angora). Christened Trappist—presumably for the monkish hue of its long coat—the cat was exhibited in 1978 under the name Cuckoo.

The breed was known simply as the Angora until June 2003, and many breeders still hang on to that word. They say a straightforward distinction between the "British Angora" and the Turkish Angora (see p.102) would be the easiest way to clear up the damaging muddle around the cat's name.

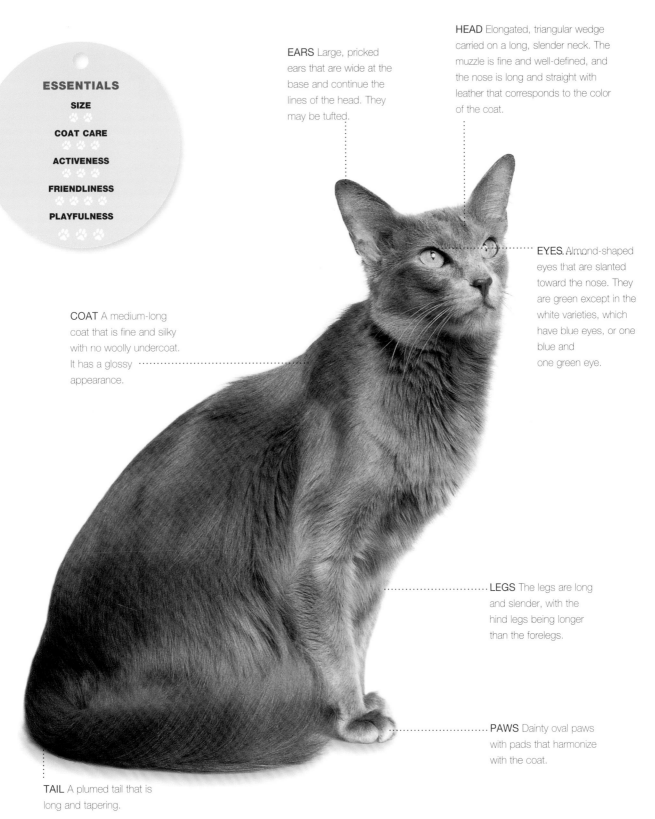

**HEAD** Elongated, triangular wedge carried on a long, slender neck. The muzzle is fine and well-defined, and the nose is long and straight with leather that corresponds to the color of the coat.

**EARS** Large, pricked ears that are wide at the base and continue the lines of the head. They may be tufted.

**ESSENTIALS**

**SIZE**

**COAT CARE**

**ACTIVENESS**

**FRIENDLINESS**

**PLAYFULNESS**

**EYES.** Almond-shaped eyes that are slanted toward the nose. They are green except in the white varieties, which have blue eyes, or one blue and one green eye.

**COAT** A medium-long coat that is fine and silky with no woolly undercoat. It has a glossy appearance.

**LEGS** The legs are long and slender, with the hind legs being longer than the forelegs.

**PAWS** Dainty oval paws with pads that harmonize with the coat.

**TAIL** A plumed tail that is long and tapering.

# Oriental Longhair

## ORIENTAL LONGHAIR FACTS

🐾 **PHYSIQUE** A medium-sized, slim cat with a long, well-muscled body.

🐾 **COAT** The Oriental Longhair is recognized in almost all colors and patterns.

🐾 **TEMPERAMENT** Gregarious and inquisitive, this is a cat that enjoys company and loves to play. It can be highly vocal in its demands.

🐾 **GROOMING** Regular brushing and stroking with a gloved hand will help to keep the coat looking its best.

Just as the shorthaired Siamese has a longhaired version in the Balinese, so the shorthaired Oriental has a longhaired version in the Oriental Longhair. It is, in effect, a cat of the Siamese type, but with a long coat in solid colors. As such, it represents the last of the four possible Oriental types.

Once the Oriental Shorthair and the Balinese had been successfully developed, there was a clear absence in the Oriental group of cat breeds: the missing cat would have to be longhaired like the Balinese, but have a coat in all the colors and patterns that had been explored in the Oriental Shorthair. The gap in the market was so obvious that it is strange that no breeder deliberately set out to fill it. The Oriental Longhair, when it eventually came about, was the result of one of those accidental matings that are the root cause of many a new breed of cat.

In 1985, an Oriental Shorthair and a Balinese at the Sholine Cattery in Houston, Texas, somehow managed to get together and mate. They produced a litter of semi-longhaired kittens, Oriental in appearance and with coats in solid colors. The owner of the cattery was a breeder named Sheryl Ann Boyle, and she immediately recognized the piece of good luck that had come her way. She used the litter to develop the Oriental Longhair. The breed was rapidly recognized by all the major registries in North America and Europe. However, it was not granted recognition by the British Governing Council of Cat Fancy because it was felt to be too similar to the breed then known as the Angora—now the Oriental Longhair (Angora).

In 1995, the American Cat Fanciers' Association decided to merge the Oriental Longhair and the Oriental Shorthair into a single breed. Many breeders of Oriental Shorthairs were unhappy to see the longhaired gene reintroduced to the breed, but the decision stood. The Oriental now encompasses more than 300 possible combinations of color, pattern, and length of fur.

**ESSENTIALS**

**SIZE**

**COAT CARE**

**ACTIVENESS**

**FRIENDLINESS**

**PLAYFULNESS**

**EYES** Medium-sized, almond-shaped that are slanted toward the nose. The color is usually green, except in the pointed and white, which has blue eyes, and the white and the bicolor, which may have blue or green eyes, or one of each color.

**COAT** Medium in length, the coat is fine and silky with no downy undercoat.

**EARS** Very large ears that are wide at the base and pointed. The tips form a triangle with the muzzle.

**TAIL** A long, thin tail that tapers to a fine point. It is covered in long hair, which forms a plume.

**HEAD** Long wedge carried on a long, slim neck. The profile is long and straight with no break in the nose, and the nose leather corresponds to the coat color.

**LEGS** The legs are long and slender, with the back legs being longer than the front ones.

**PAWS** Small, oval-shaped paws with pads that correspond to the coat color.

# Norwegian Forest Cat

## NORWEGIAN FOREST CAT FACTS

**PHYSIQUE** This is a large, sturdy, broad-chested cat that reaches maturity later than most cats, at about four years. Adult males can weigh up to 22 lb (10 kg), but females are much smaller.

**COAT** Almost all colors and patterns are acceptable.

**TEMPERAMENT** An active cat that needs to spend plenty of time outdoors, this breed is a good hunter and climber. Although independent, it enjoys human company and is good with children.

**GROOMING** The coat needs only occasional brushing and combing.

The Norwegian Forest Cat is known as a gentle giant. It has been in Scandinavia for perhaps a thousand years, but it was not until the 1970s that a planned breeding program was undertaken. In the long interim, the Norwegian Forest Cat was domesticated and made itself useful as a farmyard cat and a hunter.

It is more than possible that the Vikings played a part in the introduction of the Norwegian Forest Cat to the cold northern fringe of Europe. The Norsemen were traders as well as warriors, and were in contact with the Byzantine Empire—roughly modern-day Turkey. They may well have brought Turkish Angoras back from their travels, and if so, these may be the root stock of the thick-coated "Wegie," as it is fondly known. There is circumstantial evidence that some cats made that long journey: certain coat colors common in Turkey crop up in Norway, but rarely appear elsewhere in Europe.

The Skogkatt, as it is known in its native land, is often identified with the "fairy cat" of Norse legend. One story, which tells of a cat so hefty that even Thor—god of thunder—could not lift it, might well have been inspired by the weighty frame of the Norwegian Forest Cat. Another tale says that the wagon of Freya—goddess of love and fertility—was drawn by two big, strong cats. She would look kindly on any person who left a pan of milk in the fields for her cats to drink. There is a vestige of this tale in the Norwegian saying: "She fed the cat well," which is said of a bride if the sun shines on her wedding day.

Despite these pleasing associations, the Norwegian Forest Cat was pretty much taken for granted in its homeland until the 20th century. It was recognized as a separate breed in Norway in the 1930s, but still remained practically unknown elsewhere. It was through the efforts of one enthusiast, Carl-Frederik Norvane, that the cat was first bred seriously. It made its debut on the international stage in the 1970s, and is now exhibited worldwide.

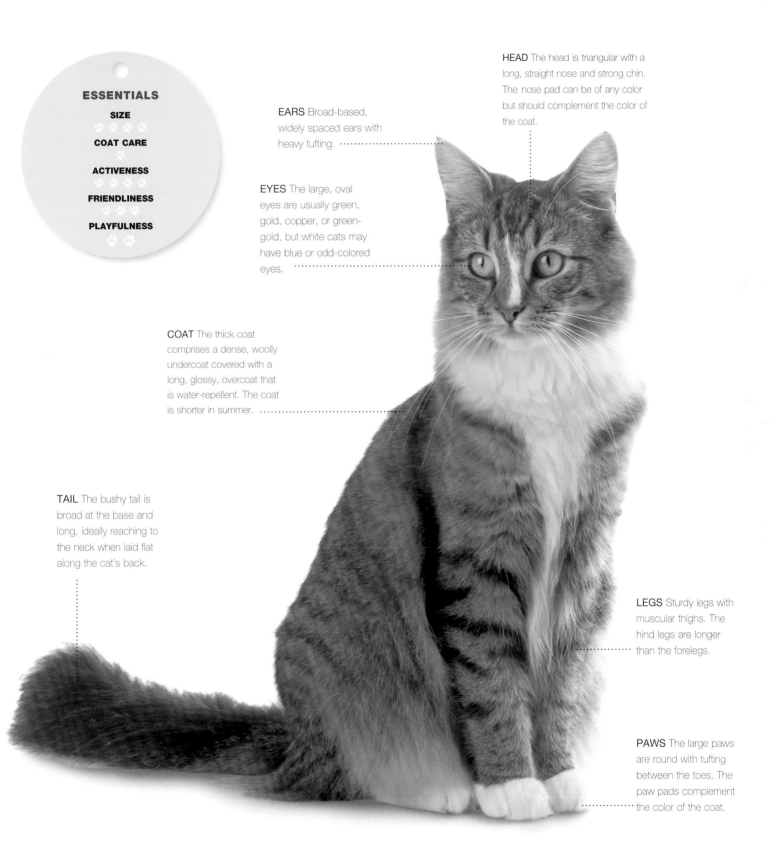

**ESSENTIALS**

SIZE

COAT CARE

ACTIVENESS

FRIENDLINESS

PLAYFULNESS

**HEAD** The head is triangular with a long, straight nose and strong chin. The nose pad can be of any color but should complement the color of the coat.

**EARS** Broad-based, widely spaced ears with heavy tufting.

**EYES** The large, oval eyes are usually green, gold, copper, or green-gold, but white cats may have blue or odd-colored eyes.

**COAT** The thick coat comprises a dense, woolly undercoat covered with a long, glossy, overcoat that is water-repellent. The coat is shorter in summer.

**TAIL** The bushy tail is broad at the base and long, ideally reaching to the neck when laid flat along the cat's back.

**LEGS** Sturdy legs with muscular thighs. The hind legs are longer than the forelegs.

**PAWS** The large paws are round with tufting between the toes. The paw pads complement the color of the coat.

# Siberian

## SIBERIAN FACTS

**PHYSIQUE** Medium to large cat with a substantial, well-muscled body.

**COAT** The Siberian comes in a wide range of colors and coat patterns, including colorpointed.

**TEMPERAMENT** An active and agile cat that is gregarious and affectionate, although it is not a lap cat. It can be chatty, and has a melodic voice.

**GROOMING** Regular combing is advised for this breed, to prevent the coat from matting.

The Siberian bears a superficial resemblance to the Maine Coon and the Norwegian Forest Cat, but it is an unrelated breed. The convergent appearance of these three is doubtless due to the similarity of the terrain and climate in which they evolved: the Siberian is clearly a cold-weather cat, built to survive in the toughest conditions.

The Siberian is something of a giant among cats. It is long and barrel-chested, and altogether rounder than the Norwegian Forest Cat with which it is so often confused. Its triple coat is dense, and beneath it there is a hefty body. But at the same time it is strong and agile: Siberians must once have been hunters, and they can make prodigious leaps and bounds when the occasion demands it. A Siberian can be taught to fetch, will pine when its owner is away, and will wag its tail when excited. For these and other reasons, it is sometimes said that the Siberian is a cat for dog people.

Russian enthusiasts claim a long history for the Siberian, and have linked it improbably with Kotofey, the Puss in Boots of Russian folklore. However, the story of the Siberian as a pedigree animal begins only with the first Russian cat shows of modern times, which took place during the glasnost era of the late-1980s. The Siberian was exhibited in Leningrad and Moscow, where it soon came to the attention of Western breeders.

Some of these novel cats were exported to Germany, where they were dubbed the Siberian Forest Cat—later shortened to Siberian. When the Siberian arrived in the United States in 1990, its somewhat feral appearance was toned down through the breeding process. But in post-communist Russia, breeders like the cats to look untamed. They see this as a truer, more natural type—and also consider it as a better expression of Russianness in what is, after all, the Russian national cat. As a result, two differing Siberian norms are evolving—one that is well-groomed and American, and one that is Russian and much wilder in appearance.

**ESSENTIALS**

SIZE

COAT CARE

ACTIVENESS

FRIENDLINESS

PLAYFULNESS

**EARS** Medium to large ears that are wide at the base with rounded tips and abundant tufting.

**EYES** The medium to large, rounded eyes are slightly slanted. They can be any color (except in the Colorpoints, which have blue eyes.)

**COAT** Triple coat that is smooth to the touch due to the slightly oily topcoat. In the ideal specimen, there should be a dense, plentiful ruff.

**LEGS** Sturdy, powerful legs.

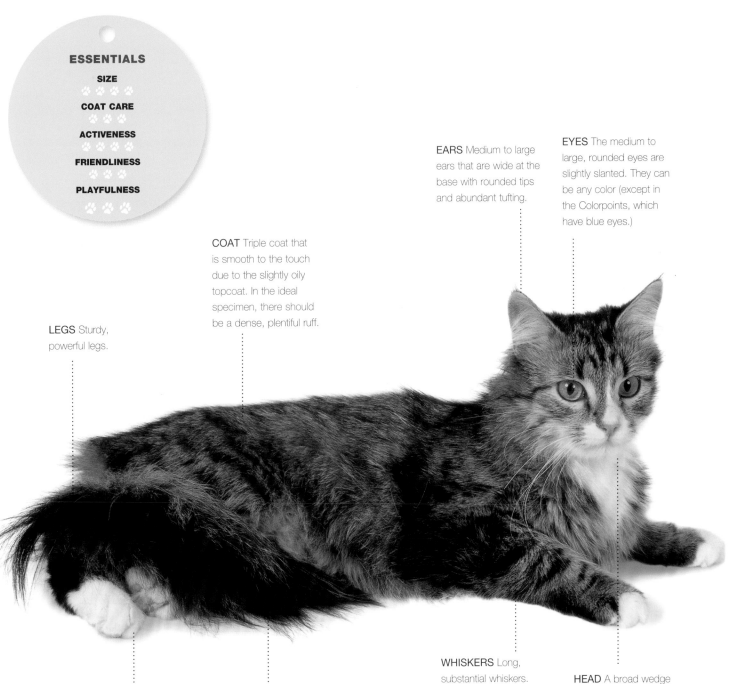

**PAWS** Large, rounded paws with toe tufts. The paw pads may not necessarily correspond to the color of the coat.

**TAIL** Medium-length bushy tail that has a blunt tip.

**WHISKERS** Long, substantial whiskers.

**HEAD** A broad wedge shape that is flat between the ears and rounded at the muzzle. The chin is in line with the nose, and the nose leather does not necessarily harmonize with the coat color.

# Birman

## BIRMAN FACTS

🐾 **PHYSIQUE** A strongly built, long-bodied cat with medium-length legs, the Birman is midway between the "cobby" and svelte body types.

🐾 **COAT** The Birman is a colorpointed cat, which comes in seal, blue, chocolate, lilac, red, and cream colors, as well as tortie and lynx (tabby) varieties.

🐾 **TEMPERAMENT** A gentle but active cat, the Birman is sociable without being demanding. It makes a good family pet, and enjoys play.

🐾 **GROOMING** Daily brushing and combing is advisable, but the coat does not easily become matted.

The strikingly marked, blue-eyed Birman is sometimes called "the sacred cat of Burma." It is not to be confused with the Burmese. The two breeds bear no relation to each other, although they do have one thing in common: both are thought to have been revered in the temples of southeast Asia.

Few cats are more thickly wreathed in myth than the Birman. Legend speaks of a temple in Burma (also known as Myanmar) where, before the time of Buddha, hundreds of pure-white cats guarded the image of a golden goddess with sapphire eyes. The temple was attacked by marauders, and at the height of the raid, the high priest, Mun-Ha, suffered a heart attack. As he lay dying, one of the cats placed its paws on his head. In that instant, the cat's eyes became blue, and its fur golden, like the goddess. Its legs and tail turned the dark color of the Burmese earth, while its feet retained the white color of Mun-Ha's hair. This miracle gave heart to the other priests, who fought off the attackers.

It is often claimed that the Birman was brought to France by two Army officers, who were given a pair by Buddhist monks during the Burmese war of 1885. But this tale is probably no less mythical than Mun-Ha's. A more likely tale states that a pair of Birmans were smuggled out of Burma in 1919. The male died en route to France, but the female was found, on arrival, to be pregnant: the Birman breed was built on the slim foundation of this one litter.

Even this last version has been questioned by some authorities, who maintain that the breed was artificially engineered in France by crossing Siamese and Persians, and that all the legends are an attempt to lend mystery to the breed. What can be said for certain is that the Birman was recognized in France in 1925, nearly died out during the Second World War, but was revived in the 1950s. The result is the good-looking, amenable cat we know today.

**ESSENTIALS**

SIZE

COAT CARE

ACTIVENESS

FRIENDLINESS

PLAYFULNESS

**EARS** A round-tipped triangle with a base that is almost as wide as it is tall.

**EYES** Widely spaced eyes that are almost perfectly round and brilliant blue in color.

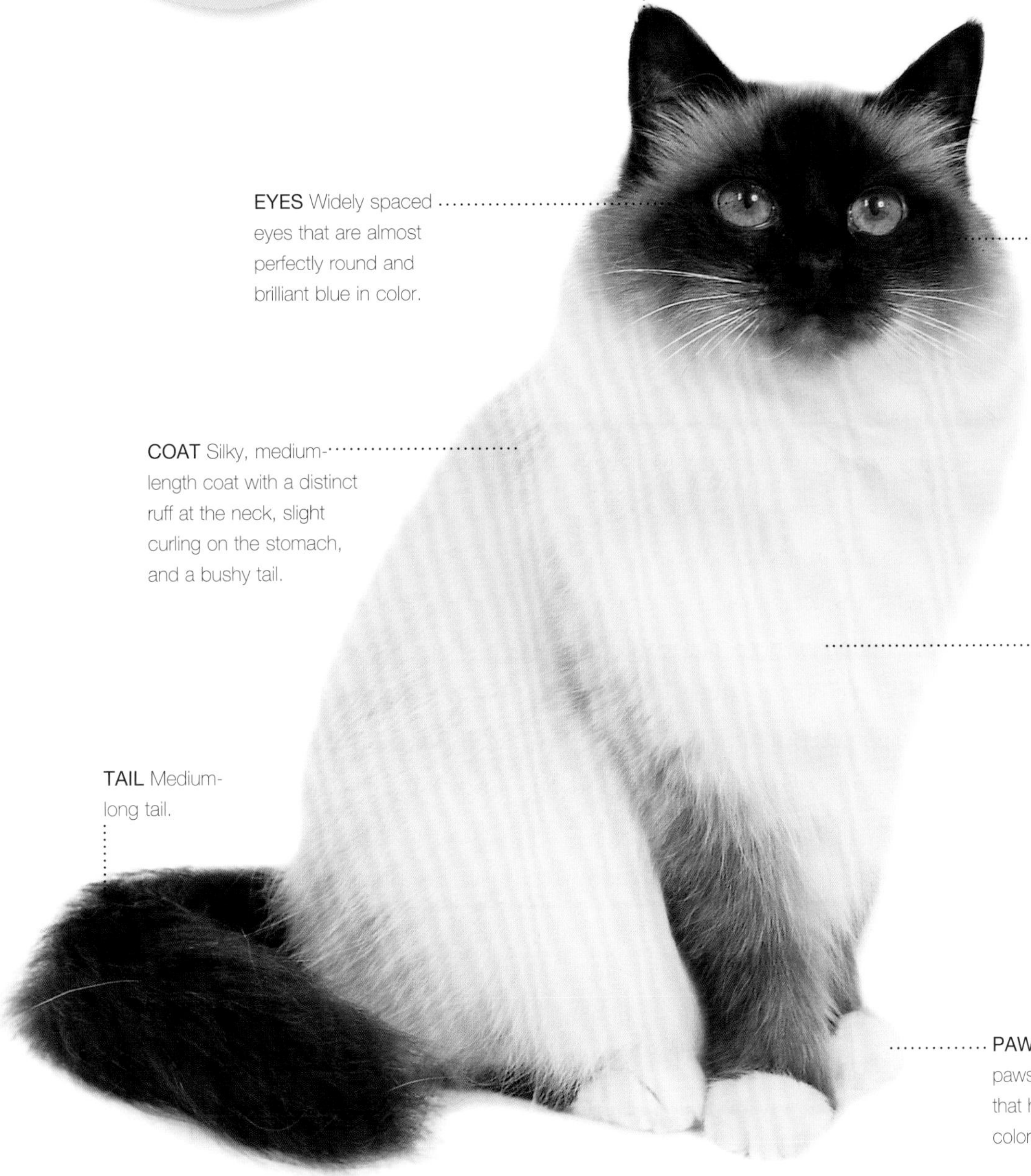

**HEAD** Rounded head with full cheeks and a slightly rounded muzzle. Longer fur at the edge of the cheeks enhances the round appearance. The medium-length nose has a slight dip, and the nose leather harmonizes with the color of the points.

**COAT** Silky, medium-length coat with a distinct ruff at the neck, slight curling on the stomach, and a bushy tail.

**COLOR** Even color on the body with contrasting dark points. There are white "gloves" on the front paws and longer "gauntlets" on the back ones. Ideally there will be a light, honey-colored cast on the back and sides but this may not be seen in kittens.

**TAIL** Medium-long tail.

**PAWS** The large, round paws are white with pads that harmonize with the color of the points.

# Ragdoll

## RAGDOLL FACTS

**PHYSIQUE** Medium to large, heavy-boned, muscular cat with a large head and broad chest.

**COAT** The three recognized patterns are bicolor, colorpoint (pale body with darker points), and mitted (as colorpoint, with a white chin, bib, chest, and feet). The colors are seal, blue, chocolate, lilac, red, and cream; points may be solid, tortie, lynx (tabby), or lynx (tabby) tortie.

**TEMPERAMENT** This is an exceedingly docile cat. Its placid nature means that it is primarily an indoor cat; it does not hunt and cannot defend itself if attacked, so should not be left outdoors on its own.

**GROOMING** The Ragdoll requires frequent combing, but the hair rarely mats.

The Ragdoll takes its name from one very peculiar characteristic: when picked up it is said to go entirely limp. At the time of its creation, this oddity created a dangerous and entirely spurious myth—that the Ragdoll does not feel pain. The controversy around the Ragdoll delayed its acceptance as a breed.

The Ragdoll is a new breed, created in 1963, and its fable is as strange as any in the canon of feline mythology. Ragdolls are said to be descended from a Persian female named Josephine, who was thought to have been hit by a car when pregnant. The kittens, when born, appeared to be insensible to pain, and exhibited the tendency to "play dead" on being taken into human arms.

From a genetic point of view, it is absurd to claim that a car accident could impart specific characteristics to a cat's unborn kittens. The only viable scientific explanation for their behavior is that a natural tendency for docility was inherited by the kittens from their mother—probably a non-pedigreed longhair—and also from their father, a Birman-type tom.

Some experts dispute even this watered-down explanation for the Ragdoll's behavior. Scientific reports commissioned by the British Governing Council of the Cat Fancy concluded that the central nervous system of the Ragdoll is in no way different from that of other cats, and that it is no more likely than any breed to go floppy or "play dead" when it is picked up. So it seems that the trait that gives the Ragdoll its name is illusory. Similarly, vets and breeders insist that the Ragdoll is as sensitive to pain as any other animal.

However, breeders and owners continue to insist that the Ragdoll is an unusually mild-mannered cat. Several variant breeds have recently been developed from the Ragdoll and have similarly gentle dispositions. The most successful of these is the RagaMuffin, which closely resembles the Ragdoll but exhibits a wider range of coat colors and patterns.

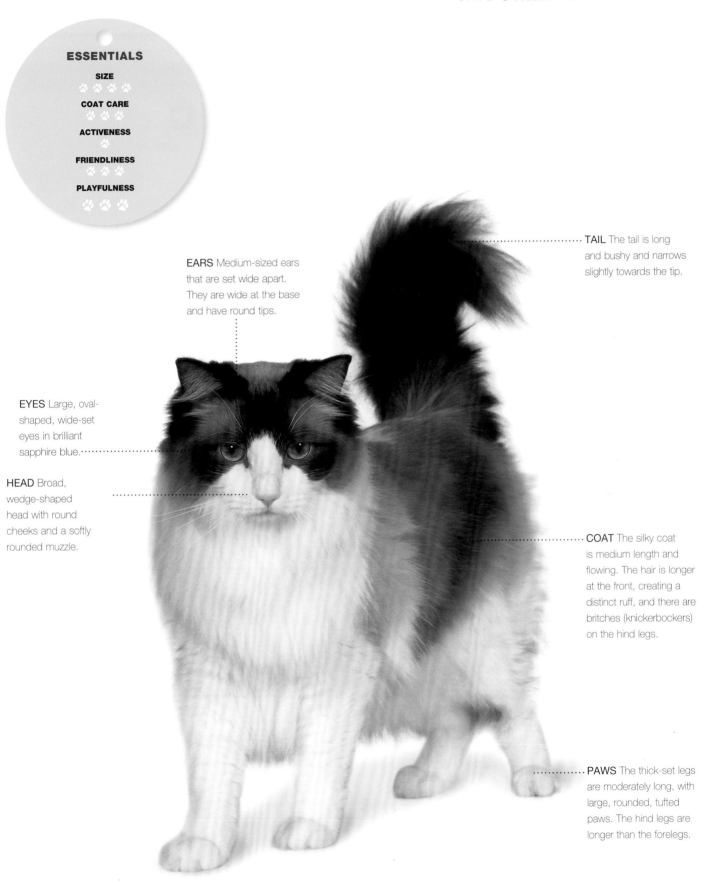

**ESSENTIALS**

SIZE

COAT CARE

ACTIVENESS

FRIENDLINESS

PLAYFULNESS

**EARS** Medium-sized ears that are set wide apart. They are wide at the base and have round tips.

**TAIL** The tail is long and bushy and narrows slightly towards the tip.

**EYES** Large, oval-shaped, wide-set eyes in brilliant sapphire blue.

**HEAD** Broad, wedge-shaped head with round cheeks and a softly rounded muzzle.

**COAT** The silky coat is medium length and flowing. The hair is longer at the front, creating a distinct ruff, and there are britches (knickerbockers) on the hind legs.

**PAWS** The thick-set legs are moderately long, with large, rounded, tufted paws. The hind legs are longer than the forelegs.

# Longhaired Exotic Variant

## LONGHAIRED EXOTIC VARIANT FACTS

**PHYSIQUE** A compact cat with broad shoulders and chest, short legs, and flattened face.

**COAT** The Longhaired Exotic Variant comes in all solid and tortie colors, as well as bicolor, shaded, smoke, tipped, colorpointed, and tabby varieties.

**TEMPERAMENT** A friendly and companiable cat. The Longhaired Exotic Variant is said to be livelier and more playful than its Persian relation.

**GROOMING** The thick coat needs daily brushing and combing.

Exotic Shorthairs are routinely bred with Persians in order to maintain the correct body type, and longhaired kittens are sometimes the result. Although longhaired, these cats cannot be registered as Persians, and nor are they true Exotic Shorthairs. They have been designated Longhaired Exotic Variants for registration purposes, but are not widely recognized.

If the Exotic is a contradictory cat—a shorthaired longhair—then this variant is even more so: it is a longhaired shorthaired longhair. This double reversal ought logically to mean that the cat is simply a Persian. And it is true that, in most ways, the Longhaired Exotic Variant is physically identical to the Persian. But for most breeders the Persian is defined by its pedigree. That is to say, genealogical history is what counts when it comes to defining a breed, not outward appearance. Some breeders claim that the Longhaired Exotic Variant is any case different in subtle ways from a true Persian. Its coat, they say, is coarser to the touch, and is not always exactly the right length. And the presence of American Shorthairs in its lineage means it tends to be rather more jumpy than the sedentary Persian.

Such fine distinctions are too much even for some registries. The International Cat Association (TICA) and the European Fédération Internationale Féline (FIFé) both allow the Longhaired Exotic to be shown as a Persian. The influential Cat Fanciers' Association and British Governing Council of the Cat Fancy, on the other hand, insist that the Longhaired Exotic is not quite the genuine Persian article.

In the end, the ins and outs of the debate matter little to anyone outside the cat-breeding community. The Longhaired Exotic Variant is still a beautiful cat, whatever appellation the governing authorities choose to give it. And many cat lovers particularly enjoy the fact that this cat delivers Persian good looks together with an outgoing and active personality.

**ESSENTIALS**

SIZE

COAT CARE

ACTIVENESS

FRIENDLINESS

PLAYFULNESS

**EYES** Large, rounded, widely-spaced eyes that give the cat a childlike appeal.

**EARS** The small, rounded ears tip slightly forward and are set low on the head, with long ear furnishings.

**COAT** Long, glossy, soft coat that stands away from the body. The hair is longer at the front, with a large ruff that continues in a frill between the front legs.

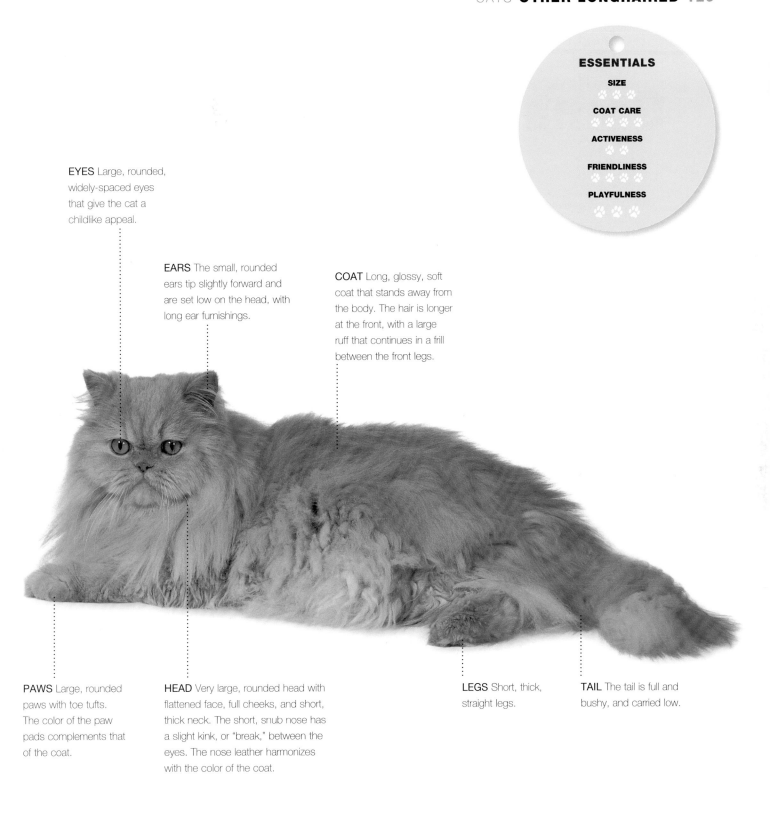

**PAWS** Large, rounded paws with toe tufts. The color of the paw pads complements that of the coat.

**HEAD** Very large, rounded head with flattened face, full cheeks, and short, thick neck. The short, snub nose has a slight kink, or "break," between the eyes. The nose leather harmonizes with the color of the coat.

**LEGS** Short, thick, straight legs.

**TAIL** The tail is full and bushy, and carried low.

# Somali

## SOMALI FACTS

🐾 **PHYSIQUE** Medium-sized cat with a long, well-proportioned body and an arched back.

🐾 **COAT** The mature Somali has a ticked, richly colored coat that comes in ruddy (usual), red (sorrel), blue, and fawn colors in the United States. Other associations accept a wider range of colors, including lilac and chocolate, tortie colors, and silver versions.

🐾 **TEMPERAMENT** An outgoing, active cat that has an innate sense of fun and a love of games. Somalis are agile and highly social.

🐾 **GROOMING** Regular brushing with a soft brush is advisable to keep the coat in good condition.

The Somali is essentially a longhaired version of the Abyssinian. Its soft and profuse red fur is strikingly attractive. The Somali can look almost vulpine, and for this reason it is sometimes called the "fox cat." Its resemblance to the fox may explain why it is often said to have a wild air about it.

Ever since Abyssinians have been systematically bred, litters have occasionally contained fuzzy little kittens that did not conform to type. These longhaired specimens may have been the result of some Persian blood that was introduced into the line early on, when thoroughbred Abyssinian stock was scarce. More likely, they are the result of a recessive gene that periodically makes its presence known. At any rate, the "shaggy" Abys were routinely excluded from breeding programs.

In 1963, a Canadian breeder named Mary Mailing exhibited a longhaired Abyssinian as a sort of joke at a show in Calgary, Canada. But one of the judges, Ken McGill, was so taken with the red-coated cat that he asked Mailing to give him one to work with. A few years later, Evelyn Mague, an American breeder of Abyssinians, became fascinated by the longhaired Abyssinians that came her

way from time to time, and began to breed specifically to produce the variant. Later she made use of some of McGill's stock.

It was Mague who coined a name for the breed. The name came about by analogy with the Balinese, which is the longhaired version of the Siamese and is so-called because Bali lies close to Siam (Thailand). Somalia borders Abyssinia (Ethiopia), so Somali seemed like a good and fitting name for the longhaired variant of the established Abyssinian shorthair.

The luxuriant coat of the Somali is a large part of its appeal. Each hair is ticked like the Aby's, but may have many more bands than the standard two or three of the Abyssinian. The Somali also has a delightful, experimental personality: it will grasp a toy between its paws, leap acrobatically, or turn on a faucet when it needs a drink.

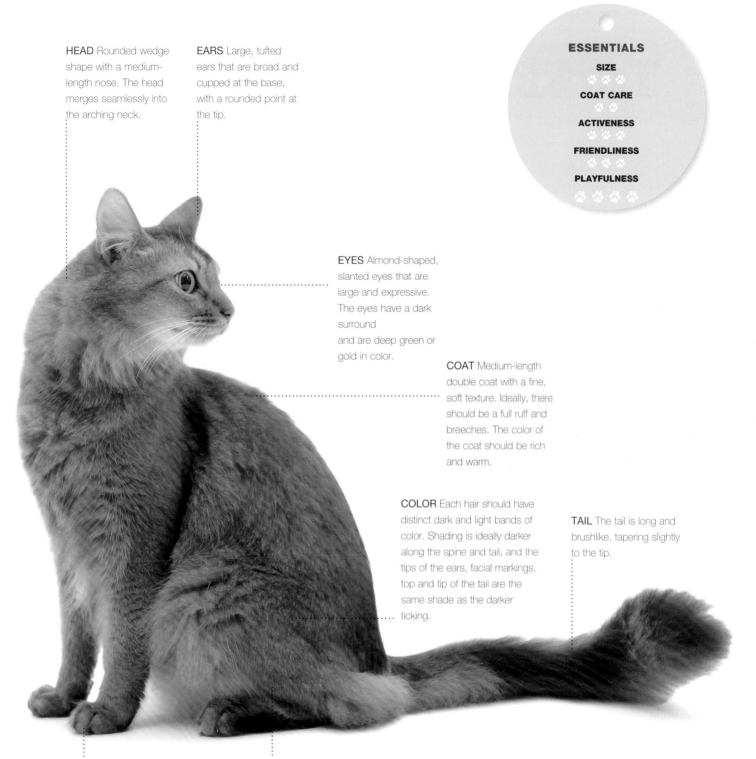

**HEAD** Rounded wedge shape with a medium-length nose. The head merges seamlessly into the arching neck.

**EARS** Large, tufted ears that are broad and cupped at the base, with a rounded point at the tip.

**ESSENTIALS**

SIZE

COAT CARE

ACTIVENESS

FRIENDLINESS

PLAYFULNESS

**EYES** Almond-shaped, slanted eyes that are large and expressive. The eyes have a dark surround and are deep green or gold in color.

**COAT** Medium-length double coat with a fine, soft texture. Ideally, there should be a full ruff and breeches. The color of the coat should be rich and warm.

**COLOR** Each hair should have distinct dark and light bands of color. Shading is ideally darker along the spine and tail, and the tips of the ears, facial markings, top and tip of the tail are the same shade as the darker ticking.

**TAIL** The tail is long and brushlike, tapering slightly to the tip.

**PAWS** Small, oval-shaped paws, with pads that complement the color of the coat.

**LEGS** Somalis stand tall on their long legs, giving the impression that they are walking on tiptoe.

# Turkish Van

## TURKISH VAN FACTS

**PHYSIQUE** Powerfully built, broad-chested, large cat with a long body.

**COAT** A white cat with colored markings restricted to the head and tail—the term "van pattern" is derived from this cat. Red (auburn) is the traditional color, but most other colors are recognized.

**TEMPERAMENT** An agile and alert cat that enjoys human contact and makes a good companion.

**GROOMING** The coat needs only occasional brushing and does not tend to mat.

The Turkish Van hails from the area around Lake Van in eastern Turkey. Its unusual markings classically consist of patches of auburn on the head and a tail of the same color. The Turkish Van has an intriguingly uncattish trait: it loves to go for swim in hot weather, hence its nickname, the Turkish swimming cat.

The snow-white coat and unique pattern of this cat attracted the attention of many visitors to Turkey in former times. It often figures as a curiosity in the paintings of Ottoman bazaars that were made by Victorian artists on their travels. Some of these cats, then as now, sported a patch of color close to the left shoulder. It was said in Turkey that this was the thumbprint of Allah, which was left on the cat when he touched it in blessing as it descended from Noah's Ark—Mount Ararat, the ark's alleged resting place, is close to the breed's native region.

It was not until the 1950s that the Turkish Van came to the attention of serious cat enthusiasts. In 1955, two English women, Laura Lushington and Sonia Halliday, took note of the Angora-like cat while vacationing close to Lake Van. They acquired a couple of specimens, and were astonished to find that the cats would happily go into water and swim way out of their depth. Lushington brought the pair back home, and was surprised once more when they bred true.

Lushington acquired more of the cats on subsequent trips to Turkey, and carried out a breeding program. The cat was registered in Great Britain in 1969 under the name Turkish Cat. In order to avoid confusion with the Turkish Angora, this was changed to the more accurate and satisfying Turkish Van.

The Turkish Van is by no means a lap cat, and the early specimens were downright aggressive. This trait has been tamed by breeding, but the Turkish Van is still independent and occasionaly nervous. It is happiest when its feet are on the ground, or in the water.

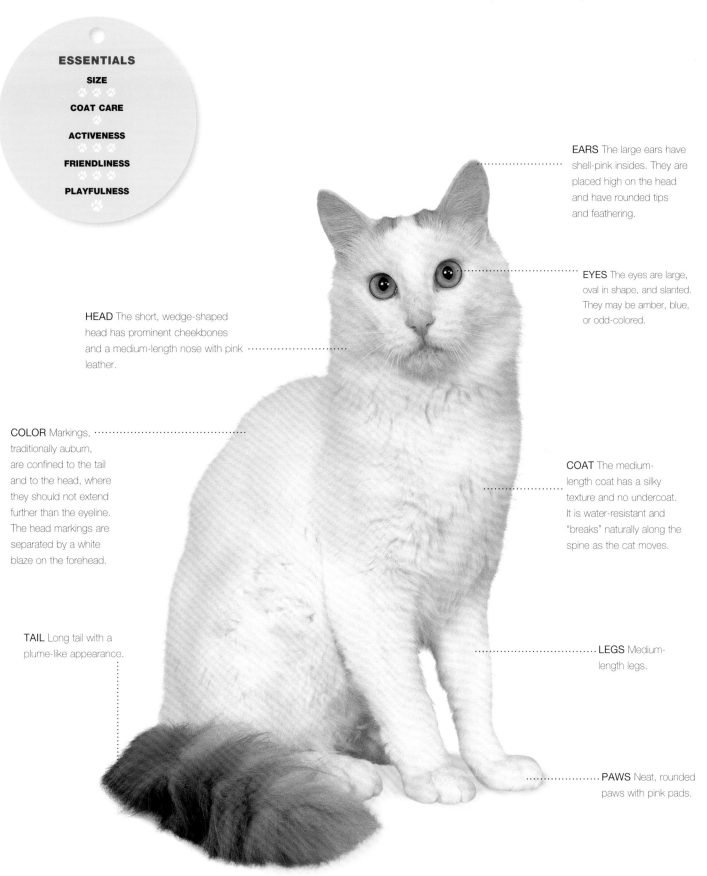

**ESSENTIALS**

SIZE

COAT CARE

ACTIVENESS

FRIENDLINESS

PLAYFULNESS

**EARS** The large ears have shell-pink insides. They are placed high on the head and have rounded tips and feathering.

**EYES** The eyes are large, oval in shape, and slanted. They may be amber, blue, or odd-colored.

**HEAD** The short, wedge-shaped head has prominent cheekbones and a medium-length nose with pink leather.

**COLOR** Markings, traditionally auburn, are confined to the tail and to the head, where they should not extend further than the eyeline. The head markings are separated by a white blaze on the forehead.

**COAT** The medium-length coat has a silky texture and no undercoat. It is water-resistant and "breaks" naturally along the spine as the cat moves.

**TAIL** Long tail with a plume-like appearance.

**LEGS** Medium-length legs.

**PAWS** Neat, rounded paws with pink pads.

# Tiffanie

## TIFFANIE FACTS

**PHYSIQUE** Slender, muscular cat with a straight back and gently rounded chest. The legs are long, slim, and elegant.

**COAT** The Tiffanie is accepted in the following self (solid) and tortie colors: black, blue, chocolate, lilac, red, cream, caramel, apricot (self only), and the silver versions of these colors. There are also shaded Tiffanies.

**TEMPERAMENT** This cat has a calm yet sociable personality, and so makes a good companion.

**GROOMING** Regular brushing with a soft brush is needed.

The Tiffanie is a British breed that is—understandably—often confused with the American-produced Tiffany (also known as the Chantilly). The confusion goes right back to the foundation of the breed, but the bare facts of the matter are that the Tiffanie is a longhaired Burmese. It is also the only longhaired member of the Asian group.

The Tiffanie shares its ancestry with the Burmilla. Both breeds can be traced back to a chance mating that took place in 1981 between a Lilac Burmese female and a Chinchilla Persian male. The cats in question belonged to Baroness Miranda von Kirchberg, a well-known breeder of Russian Blues. The four kittens born to the Lilac Burmese turned out to be silver-shaded females. Von Kirchberg thought they could be used to create a new breed, and embarked on a program to create silver-shaded shorthaired Burmese. These are the cats that came to be known as Burmillas.

But the program also produced some semi-longhaired shaded Burmese. Further matings produced self-colored longhaired Burmese. The brown ones were very similar to the breed already known in the United States as the Tiffany, and at the time it was wrongly supposed in the UK that the longhaired American Tiffany was also derived from the Burmese. It was therefore proposed to give the British longhaired Burmese the same name. But it turned out that the word "Tiffany" was already registered as a breeder's prefix, and so could not be used as a breed name in Britain.

The creators of the longhaired Burmese dodged the issue by merely adapting the spelling of the word—Tiffanie rather than Tiffany—thinking it would be clear to the world that they were the same cat. So it is ironic that the Tiffany and the Tiffanie turned out to be genetically quite distinct. The American Tiffany has no trace of Burmese in its background, and the name "Tiffanie" is a false homage. Unfortunately, the rebranding of the American Tiffany as the Chantilly did little to clear up the confusion, which persists to this day.

**ESSENTIALS**

SIZE

COAT CARE

ACTIVENESS

FRIENDLINESS

PLAYFULNESS

**EARS** Medium to large, broad-based ears that have rounded tips and abundant feathering. They are set well apart and are tilted slightly forward.

**EYES** Large, wide-set, expressive eyes of yellow through to green—gold is the preferred color.

**HEAD** Short wedge with a distinct break in the nose and a blunt muzzle. The nose is straight and the tip aligns with the tip of the chin when viewed in profile. The nose leather complements the color of the coat.

**COAT** Medium-long silky coat with a glossy appearance. Ideally there should be a full ruff and britches.

**TAIL** Plume-like, medium to long tail with a rounded tip, carried proudly upright.

**LEGS** Long, slender legs that end in neat, oval paws. The paw pads complement the color of the coat.

# Cats with other Special Features

Some of the most striking cats are those with unusual physical features: spotted coats, curled ears, bobbed tails. Many of these characteristics are the result of a chance mutation that a breeder has noticed and perpetuated: the hairless Sphynx, the flop-eared Scottish Fold, and the wavy-haired Rex are all such breeds. Some unusual features have been deliberately engineered in order to create a specific look. Among such cats are the California Spangled and the Ocicat, both of which have been bred to resemble wild feline species.

# Cornish Rex

## CORNISH REX FACTS

**PHYSIQUE** A medium-sized cat that has a slender but muscular body and a long, elegant neck.

**COAT** All colors and patterns are recognized.

**TEMPERAMENT** A naturally extrovert and affectionate cat, the Cornish Rex is exceptionally playful. It is very active and is a good jumper.

**GROOMING** Hand grooming is usually all that is needed to keep the coat looking good.

The Cornish Rex is a result of a spontaneous genetic mutation that occurred in Cornwall, southwest England, in 1950. A white female farm cat gave birth to a litter that contained a tabby with hair that was tightly curled. The cat, named Kallibunker, became the founding father of this extrovert breed.

The genetic mutation that leads to curly coats is not just confined to cats. Kallibunker's owner, Nina Ennismore, immediately recognized that the kitten's oddly waved hair was similar to the so-called "rex mutation" that is sometimes observed in rabbits. Ennismore borrowed the rabbit fanciers' term, and so the new breed came to be called the Cornish Rex.

At the suggestion of the local vet, Kallibunker was mated back to his mother. This strategy produced two more curly kittens. But the fact that the gene pool was so restricted (Kallibunker's parents may also have been closely related) meant that the kittens born in the next couple of generations were not always in the best health. It was soon clear that the only way to establish the "rex gene" was to outcross to other breeds.

One fourth-generation rexed kitten was exported to the United States in 1957, where it was crossed with Oriental Shorthairs and Siamese. In Britain, meanwhile, the best Cornish Rex specimens were crossed with British Shorthairs and Burmese. Both programs were successful, but the result was two slightly differing physiques for the cat on either side of the Atlantic: the American variant is more delicate than the British, and displays a very clearly "arched" torso.

Yet the American and UK versions share the same "washboard" coat, the silky feel of which is most apparent on the back and tail. The extraordinary texture of the Cornish Rex's fur is due not just to its curliness, but also to the fact that it has no guard hairs. The rex gene makes for what is, in effect, an incomplete coat.

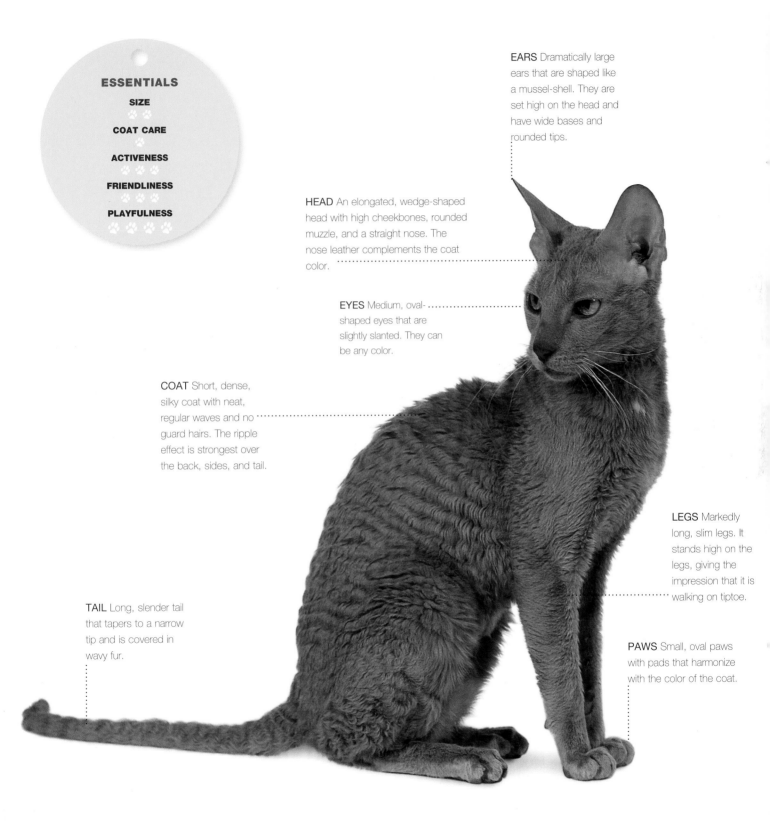

**ESSENTIALS**

SIZE

COAT CARE

ACTIVENESS

FRIENDLINESS

PLAYFULNESS

**EARS** Dramatically large ears that are shaped like a mussel-shell. They are set high on the head and have wide bases and rounded tips.

**HEAD** An elongated, wedge-shaped head with high cheekbones, rounded muzzle, and a straight nose. The nose leather complements the coat color.

**EYES** Medium, oval-shaped eyes that are slightly slanted. They can be any color.

**COAT** Short, dense, silky coat with neat, regular waves and no guard hairs. The ripple effect is strongest over the back, sides, and tail.

**LEGS** Markedly long, slim legs. It stands high on the legs, giving the impression that it is walking on tiptoe.

**TAIL** Long, slender tail that tapers to a narrow tip and is covered in wavy fur.

**PAWS** Small, oval paws with pads that harmonize with the color of the coat.

# Devon Rex

## DEVON REX FACTS

🐾 **PHYSIQUE** This striking cat has a fine-boned but muscular body with long, sturdy legs. Its prominent cheekbones and oversized eyes and ears give it an elfin appearance.

🐾 **COAT** All colors and patterns are accepted. The smoke variety shows off the wavy fur to the best advantage.

🐾 **TEMPERAMENT** A very lively, playful cat. Devon Rexes are good jumpers. They are highly inquisitive, sociable, and chatty.

🐾 **GROOMING** Regular, gentle stroking with a gloved hand is all that is needed to maintain the coat in good condition.

Two characteristics make this such an outlandish cat. One is its coat, which is rippled like a set of ruched curtains. The other is its remarkable face: the Devon Rex has a tiny head with great round eyes, huge bat-ears, and a bemused expression, often described as "pixie-like." Its strange, almost other-worldly appearance helped to land this breed a role in the sci-fi film *Dune*.

The Devon Rex, like the Cornish Rex, came about as the result of genetic mutation. In 1960, a feral tom with curly hair was spotted living near a tin-mine in Buckfastleigh in the English county of Devon. Numerous attempts were made to catch the cat and breed from him, but he always managed to dodge his pursuers. He did, however, mate with a female stray who was less wary of humankind. That cat's litter was born in the garden of an animal welfare worker named Beryl Cox, and one of the kittens had the same rexed coat as his elusive father. Miss Cox adopted the kitten and named him Kirlee.

The Cornish Rex had arisen in the neighbouring county of Cornwall only ten years before, and at first it was assumed that the Devon Rex was the same breed. But when Devon Rexes were mated with Cornish Rexes, they produced only straight-haired cats—proof positive that the mutation that produced the curly coat was different in each case. In other words, the Cornish Rex and the Devon Rex were genetically distinct breeds; the fact that they arose in the same corner of the world was pure coincidence. This was readily accepted in Britain, where the Devon Rex was recognized in 1967; yet in the United States, the two breeds were treated as one until the end of the 1970s.

As it happens, the two breeds' similarity in appearance is merely superficial. The Devon Rex alone has the almost unnerving facial characteristics that have earned it the nickname "the alien cat." Its fur is also coarser and thinner than that of its neighbour. Not for nothing is it also sometimes called "the Poodle cat".

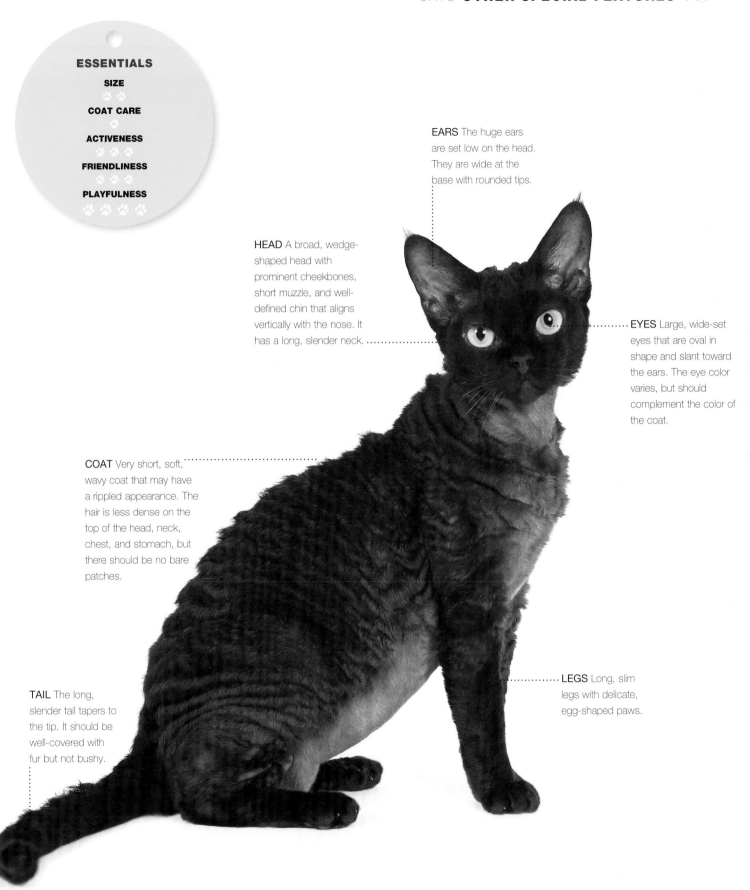

**ESSENTIALS**

SIZE

COAT CARE

ACTIVENESS

FRIENDLINESS

PLAYFULNESS

**EARS** The huge ears are set low on the head. They are wide at the base with rounded tips.

**HEAD** A broad, wedge-shaped head with prominent cheekbones, short muzzle, and well-defined chin that aligns vertically with the nose. It has a long, slender neck.

**EYES** Large, wide-set eyes that are oval in shape and slant toward the ears. The eye color varies, but should complement the color of the coat.

**COAT** Very short, soft, wavy coat that may have a rippled appearance. The hair is less dense on the top of the head, neck, chest, and stomach, but there should be no bare patches.

**TAIL** The long, slender tail tapers to the tip. It should be well-covered with fur but not bushy.

**LEGS** Long, slim legs with delicate, egg-shaped paws.

# Shorthair LaPerm

## SHORTHAIR LAPERM FACTS

**PHYSIQUE** Medium-sized, muscular cat which feels surprisingly heavy for its size.

**COAT** All colors and patterns are accepted.

**TEMPERAMENT** An exceptionally loving and playful cat that will follow its owner and come when called, like a dog. It is an excellent hunter.

**GROOMING** Occasional baths followed by towel-drying will maintain the curl (blow-drying can make the hair frizz). Only minimal combing is needed.

The LaPerm is one of the newer breeds of cat. It is the result of a random genetic mutation that appeared in a farm cat in 1982. The cat's distinctive feature is its unusual rexed coat, which takes the form of very tight curls. But beneath the luxuriant fur is the lean body of a hunting cat.

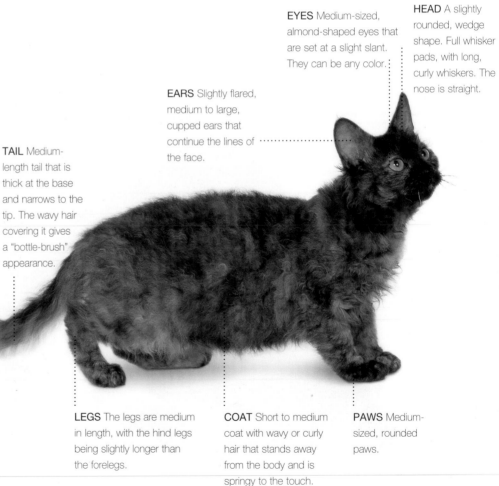

**EYES** Medium-sized, almond-shaped eyes that are set at a slight slant. They can be any color.

**HEAD** A slightly rounded, wedge shape. Full whisker pads, with long, curly whiskers. The nose is straight.

**EARS** Slightly flared, medium to large, cupped ears that continue the lines of the face.

**TAIL** Medium-length tail that is thick at the base and narrows to the tip. The wavy hair covering it gives a "bottle-brush" appearance.

**LEGS** The legs are medium in length, with the hind legs being slightly longer than the forelegs.

**COAT** Short to medium coat with wavy or curly hair that stands away from the body and is springy to the touch.

**PAWS** Medium-sized, rounded paws.

### ESSENTIALS

**SIZE**

**COAT CARE**

**ACTIVENESS**

**FRIENDLINESS**

**PLAYFULNESS**

# Longhair LaPerm

The original LaPerm was a shorthaired cat. It proved easy to breed and it was only a matter of time before a longhaired variant was produced. The Longhair LaPerm has a mass of fine curls, which are so light that the coat parts when you blow it. It can appear almost unkempt—a look dubbed the "Gypsy Shag."

**HEAD** A slightly rounded, wedge shape. Full whisker pads, with long, curly whiskers. The nose is straight.

**EARS** Slightly flared, cupped ears that continue the lines of the face. They are medium to large in size, and may have curly hair on the insides.

**COAT** Medium-long, loose, bouncy coat that stands away from the body and has a springy, textured feel. The fur at the neck, ruff, and base of the ear has the tightest and longest curls. There are seasonal changes in the length and fullness of the coat.

**EYES** Medium-sized, almond-shaped eyes that are set at a slight slant. They can be any color.

**TAIL** Plumed, medium-sized tail that is thick at the base and narrows to the tip.

**LEGS** The legs are medium in length, with the hind legs being slightly longer than the forelegs.

**PAWS** Medium-sized, rounded paws.

## LONGHAIR LAPERM FACTS

**PHYSIQUE** Medium-sized, muscular cat that feels surprisingly heavy for its size.

**COAT** All colors and patterns are accepted.

**TEMPERAMENT** This is an exceptionally loving, playful cat that will follow its owner and come when called. The LaPerm is an excellent hunter.

**GROOMING** Occasional baths followed by towel-drying will maintain the curl (blow-drying can make the hair frizz). Only minimal combing is needed.

### ESSENTIALS

SIZE

COAT CARE

ACTIVENESS

FRIENDLINESS

PLAYFULNESS

# Shorthair Selkirk Rex

## SHORTHAIR SELKIRK REX FACTS

🐾 **PHYSIQUE** A medium to large cat with a heavy-boned, "cobby" frame and a straight rather than arched back. The legs are sturdy and medium in length.

🐾 **COAT** All colors and patterns are accepted.

🐾 **TEMPERAMENT** An alert and active cat with a sweet and laidback disposition. It is undemanding and can happily amuse itself, but still enjoys attention when its owner is available.

🐾 **GROOMING** An occasional bath and weekly combing is required to keep the coat in top condition.

The Selkirk Rex derives from an American kitten born in 1987 that was extravagantly called Miss DePesto of NoFace. "Pest" was the only cat in a litter of seven to have curly hair, but went on to produce three curly-haired kittens that were used to found the breed. The breed was named Selkirk Rex after the Selkirk Mountains that are close to Pest's birthplace.

The Selkirk Rex is a very new breed meaning that its breeding history has been well documented, with the origins resting with just one breeder in the USA. Jeri Newman, a Persian breeder with an interest in feline genetics, adopted 'Pest' believing the kitten to be related to another Rex breed, such as the Cornish or Devon Rex.

After a bit of experimenting it became apparent that Pest's mutation that gave her and her litter their distinctive curly hair was actually a dominant gene, and she was also carrying the recessive long hair gene. Currently, all Selkirk Rex cats can be traced back to Miss DePesto. The Selkirk Rex arrived in Britain in 2002 from Austria, where it gained preliminary breed recognition in 2003, and full championship status six years later.

Undoubtedly, the defining feature of this breed is its unusual coat which can either be long or short. The shorthaired variety has quite tufty fur, although it is generally the same length all over the body. The ruff and tail hairs are the same length as the rest of the body, although the plush, curly coat on the tail lies flat against the tail.

This breed is sociable, enjoying the company of humans or other cats. This breed behaves like a lap cat and appreciates cuddles and affection from its owner. It is a laidback cat but can be inquisitive and will enjoy playing well into adulthood – be sure not to leave this cat alone for prolonged periods of time.

**EARS** Medium-sized, broad-based ears that are widely placed on the head. They may have tufts at the tips, and curly internal furnishings.

**HEAD** Broad and rounded head with full cheeks. It is carried on a short, thick neck. Full whisker pad, with long, curly whiskers. The tip of the chin aligns with the tip of the curved nose.

**EYES** Round, open eyes that are large in size and widely spaced. They can be any color.

**COAT** Soft, thick coat that stands away from the body and makes loose, curls that form random clumps rather than a regular wave pattern. The curls are tightest on the neck, underbelly, and tail.

**LEGS** Heavy-boned legs with rounded paws.

**TAIL** Thick tail that tapers to a rounded tip, and is covered in plush curls.

**ESSENTIALS**

SIZE

COAT CARE

ACTIVENESS

FRIENDLINESS

PLAYFULNESS

# Longhair Selkirk Rex

## LONGHAIR SELKIRK REX FACTS

**PHYSIQUE** Medium to large cat with a heavy-boned, "cobby" frame and straight rather than arched back. The legs are sturdy and medium in length.

**COAT** All colors and patterns are accepted.

**TEMPERAMENT** An alert and active cat with a sweet and laidback disposition. It is undemanding and can happily amuse itself, but still enjoys attention when its owner is available.

**GROOMING** An occasional bath and regular, gentle combing is needed to maintain the smooth curls of the coat.

Probably the most eye-catching of all rexed cats, the Longhair Selkirk Rex's long, loose ringlets create a thick, shaggy coat that invites you to touch it. Other rexed breeds tend toward the Oriental shape, but the Selkirk is being bred as a large, "cobby" type rather like the British Shorthair. It also shares that cat's calm disposition.

The Longhaired Selkirk Rex is a variation of the shorthaired Selkirk Rex, with both variations developed from 'Miss DePesto', the cat who began the curly haired breed. The long-haired version has a wonderful texture, especially when it is the result of parents with the rex gene and the straight-haired gene as this produces the famous ringlet texture.

With this breed, the curly hair is apparent in kittens although this may shed before re-appearing in young adulthood. It can take up to two years for the coat to fully develop into the shaggy, cuddly fur that the Selkirk is known for. In a showing environment, kittens and young adults are judged on head and body shape since their coats have not yet fully developed. The head should be rounded, with medium-sized ears sitting erect on top of the head. The ears may have tufts at the tips, and curly internal fur. With this breed, the eye colour is not determined by the coat colour, and is accepted in any shade. The body is a round 'cobby' type, with a level back and muscular torso.

The Selkirk Rex is often affectionately referred to as the 'teddy-bear' of cats, or 'the cat in sheep's clothing' as it is referred to in America. A laidback cat, the Selkirk Rex will not object to cuddling but also enjoys activity and will happily amuse himself.

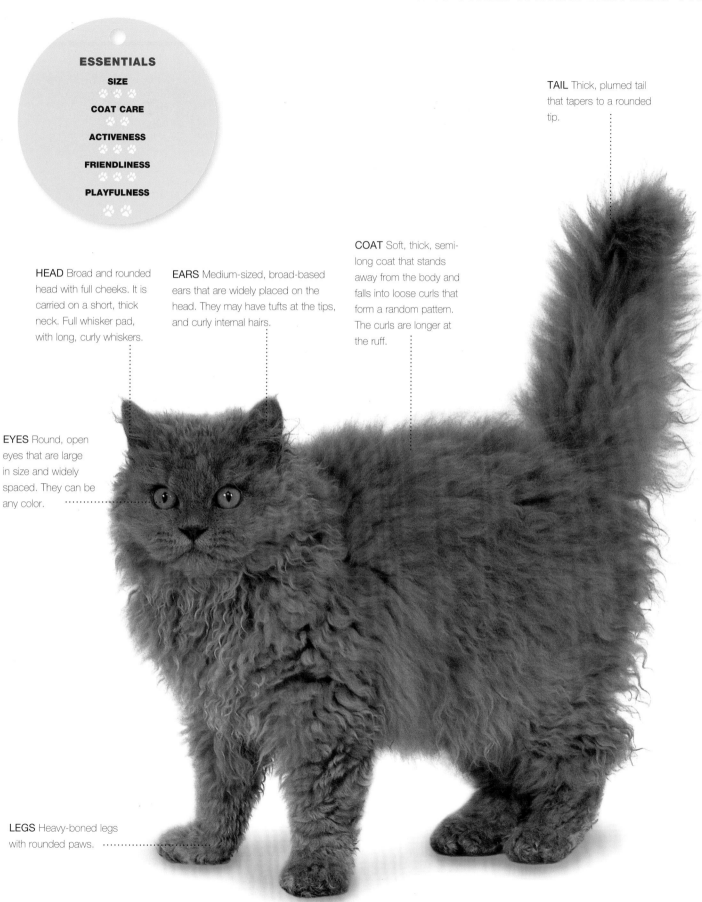

**ESSENTIALS**

**SIZE**

**COAT CARE**

**ACTIVENESS**

**FRIENDLINESS**

**PLAYFULNESS**

**TAIL** Thick, plumed tail that tapers to a rounded tip.

**HEAD** Broad and rounded head with full cheeks. It is carried on a short, thick neck. Full whisker pad, with long, curly whiskers.

**EARS** Medium-sized, broad-based ears that are widely placed on the head. They may have tufts at the tips, and curly internal hairs.

**COAT** Soft, thick, semi-long coat that stands away from the body and falls into loose curls that form a random pattern. The curls are longer at the ruff.

**EYES** Round, open eyes that are large in size and widely spaced. They can be any color.

**LEGS** Heavy-boned legs with rounded paws.

# California Spangled

## CALIFORNIA SPANGLED FACTS

🐾 **PHYSIQUE** Medium-sized cat with a long, muscular body. The legs are low, but appear shorter as they carry the body low—in a typical hunting gait.

🐾 **COAT** The California Spangled is a spotted tabby that comes in black, charcoal, brown, bronze, red, blue, gold, and silver.

🐾 **TEMPERAMENT** An athletic cat that enjoys play and has good hunting instincts. The California Spangled is gregarious and loving.

🐾 **GROOMING** Occasional brushing is all that is needed to keep the coat looking good.

The California Spangled Cat is unique in that it was bred for the specific purpose of making a point about wildlife conservation. With its spotted coat and its low-slung hunter's gait, it looks like a wild animal itself, but (unlike the Bengal) there is not a drop of wildcat blood in its line.

The California Spangled is the creation of an American screenwriter named Paul Casey. In 1971 he was working on a project in the Olduvai Gorge in Tanzania. While there, he was shocked to hear of the widespread destruction of big cats in the area. It occurred to Casey that people in the West would be far less inclined to wear leopard and other furs and skins if they mentally connected the garments with the living animal.

So he resolved to use entirely domestic stock to create a breed of cat that looked like the spotted big cats of the African savannah. He drew up a plan to engineer the cat over eleven generations and using eight different lines: Siamese, Angoras, British Shorthairs, American Shorthairs, Manx, Abyssinians, and—toward the end of the process—a muscular shorthair from Malaysia, and a spotted street cat from Cairo.

Amazingly, this strange and complex genetic recipe yielded the first true California Spangled cats in the eleventh generation, just as Casey had intended. Casey introduced the new cat not at a show, but in the pages of the Neiman Marcus Christmas mail-order catalog. The cats were advertized as "his and hers" gifts and priced at US$1,400 each. Critics pointed out that the same catalog featured a range of fur coats (but Casey would surely have argued that the whole point was to market the cat to people who might be tempted to buy such things, to potentially change their ways of thinking).

In the event, Casey got far more orders than he could fill. Demand depleted his stock and so slowed the breeding program. Ironically or fittingly, the California Spangled became as rare and precious as the big cats it was bred to resemble.

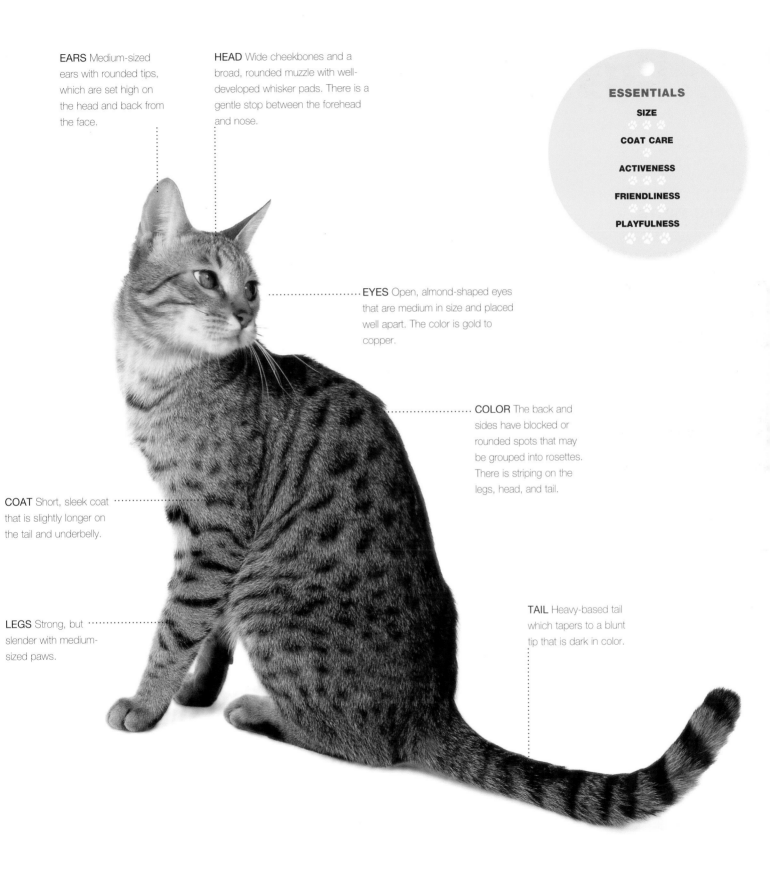

**EARS** Medium-sized ears with rounded tips, which are set high on the head and back from the face.

**HEAD** Wide cheekbones and a broad, rounded muzzle with well-developed whisker pads. There is a gentle stop between the forehead and nose.

**ESSENTIALS**

**SIZE**

**COAT CARE**

**ACTIVENESS**

**FRIENDLINESS**

**PLAYFULNESS**

**EYES** Open, almond-shaped eyes that are medium in size and placed well apart. The color is gold to copper.

**COLOR** The back and sides have blocked or rounded spots that may be grouped into rosettes. There is striping on the legs, head, and tail.

**COAT** Short, sleek coat that is slightly longer on the tail and underbelly.

**LEGS** Strong, but slender with medium-sized paws.

**TAIL** Heavy-based tail which tapers to a blunt tip that is dark in color.

# Egyptian Mau

## MAU FACTS

**PHYSIQUE** A medium-sized, muscular cat with high and prominent shoulder blades. The females are more delicate than the males.

**COAT** Silver, bronze, and smoke are the three varieties recognized for showing. There are also black and blue versions.

**TEMPERAMENT** The Egyptian Mau tends to attach itself to one or two people, making it a loyal and affectionate pet. It is playful and easy to train.

**GROOMING** Regular brushing is advised to maintain the coat.

Mau is the Egyptian word for "cat," which is fitting for a breed descended from the street cats of Cairo. The only natural spotted domestic cat, its unusual coat pattern is similar to paintings of cats on ancient Egyptians scrolls and murals. The gooseberry-green eyes and distinctive mascara lines are what gives the Silver Egyptian Mau its characteristically worried appearance.

The modern history of the Egyptian Mau begins not in Cairo but in Rome. In 1953, an expatriate Russian princess, Natalie Troubetskoy, conceived a strong liking for two spotted cats belonging to the Egyptian ambassador to Italy. He was a friend of hers, and he helped her to get a similar female from Egypt. The newly acquired queen was mated with the ambassador's tom. This and subsequent crosses produced the founding stock of the breed. Trubetskoy exhibited a Mau in Italy in 1955, but emigrated to America soon after, taking her Maus with her. One of them was exhibited in the United States in 1957. Official recognition of the breed came in 1977.

In Britain, meanwhile, a breeder named Angela Sayer had set herself the task of artificially recreating the cat seen in ancient Egyptian art. Independently of Princess Troubetskoy, she decided to call it a Mau—a coincidence that has caused much confusion down the years. The cat that Sayer eventually produced was, in effect, a Siamese with a spotted-tabby coat and, ironically enough, it bears a closer resemblance to the ancient Egyptian cat than does the Mau derived from genuine Egyptian street cats. To distinguish it from the Egyptian Mau, the British-made cat is now called the Oriental Spotted Tabby.

The Egyptian Mau has largely been confined to the United States, where it is very popular. Two quirks of character set it apart from other cats. It is extremely swift, perhaps the fastest-running cat in the world. It also seems to enjoy being walked on a leash—a faint echo, perhaps, of its erstwhile status as the court pet of the pharaohs.

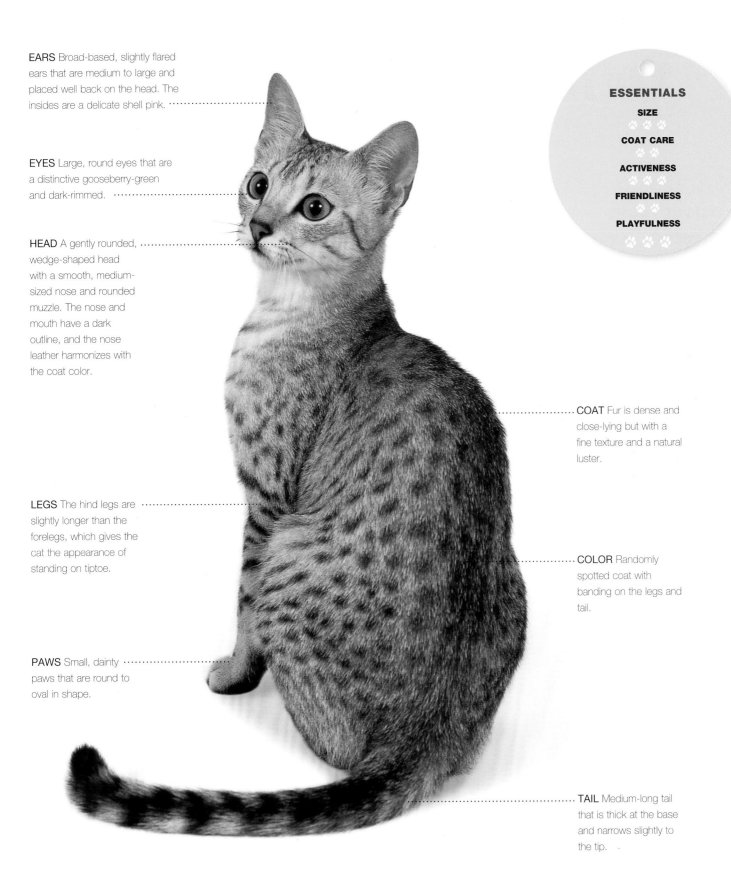

**EARS** Broad-based, slightly flared ears that are medium to large and placed well back on the head. The insides are a delicate shell pink.

**EYES** Large, round eyes that are a distinctive gooseberry-green and dark-rimmed.

**HEAD** A gently rounded, wedge-shaped head with a smooth, medium-sized nose and rounded muzzle. The nose and mouth have a dark outline, and the nose leather harmonizes with the coat color.

**LEGS** The hind legs are slightly longer than the forelegs, which gives the cat the appearance of standing on tiptoe.

**PAWS** Small, dainty paws that are round to oval in shape.

**ESSENTIALS**

SIZE

COAT CARE

ACTIVENESS

FRIENDLINESS

PLAYFULNESS

**COAT** Fur is dense and close-lying but with a fine texture and a natural luster.

**COLOR** Randomly spotted coat with banding on the legs and tail.

**TAIL** Medium-long tail that is thick at the base and narrows slightly to the tip.

# Ocicat

## OCICAT FACTS

**PHYSIQUE** Large, athletic cat with a long, solid body, muscular chest, and naturally wild appearance.

**COAT** Tawny (brown spotted tabby), chocolate, cinnamon, blue, lavender (lilac), and fawn. There are also silver versions of the same colors.

**TEMPERAMENT** The Ocicat is friendly and can exhibit a doglike loyalty to its carers. It responds well to training, and may enjoy walking on a leash or playing "fetch."

**GROOMING** Regular brushing or stroking with a silk cloth helps bring out the sheen of the coat.

The Ocicat is so-called for its uncanny resemblance to the ocelot, which is itself the most feline in appearance of all the wildcats. The Ocicat bears no genetic relation to the ocelot, however. Its beautiful spotted coat is the chance outcome of a breeding program intended to yield an altogether different look.

Breeding is an inexact science, and several established cat breeds are the result of an unexpected outcome, a lucky spin of the genetic wheel. The Ocicat is one such animal. In the 1960s, a breeder named Virginia Daly of Michigan was crossing Siamese cats with Abyssinians in the expectation of producing Aby-pointed Siamese kittens. She succeeded, but in the second generation she also found that she had a male kitten with golden spots. She called it Tonga, but her daughter noticed that it looked very like a baby ocelot, and so dubbed it the Ocicat.

Since Tonga was not of use to the breeding program, he was neutered and sold to a student for US$10. And that might have been the end of the line for the Ocicat, had not Mrs Daly mentioned his existence to a fellow breeder named Clyde Keeler, who was interested in producing a cat similar to the extinct Egyptian Spotted Fishing Cat. Keeler saw that Tonga was a step toward that goal, and was disappointed to learn that he had been neutered. But his enthusiasm rekindled Mrs Daly's interest in the spotted cat. She managed to produce another—this time a female that was named Dalai Talua. This she-cat was to be the founder of the breed.

Other breeders took the Ocicat on, and strengthened the stock by introducing American Shorthairs into the bloodline. This also had the effect of increasing the Ocicat's size: it is quite a large animal—a trait which, together with its wildcat markings, make it look less than tame. But the Ocicat's dangerous good looks belie its true nature: it is as friendly and sweet-tempered a cat as any you will find.

**ESSENTIALS**

SIZE

COAT CARE

ACTIVENESS

FRIENDLINESS

PLAYFULNESS

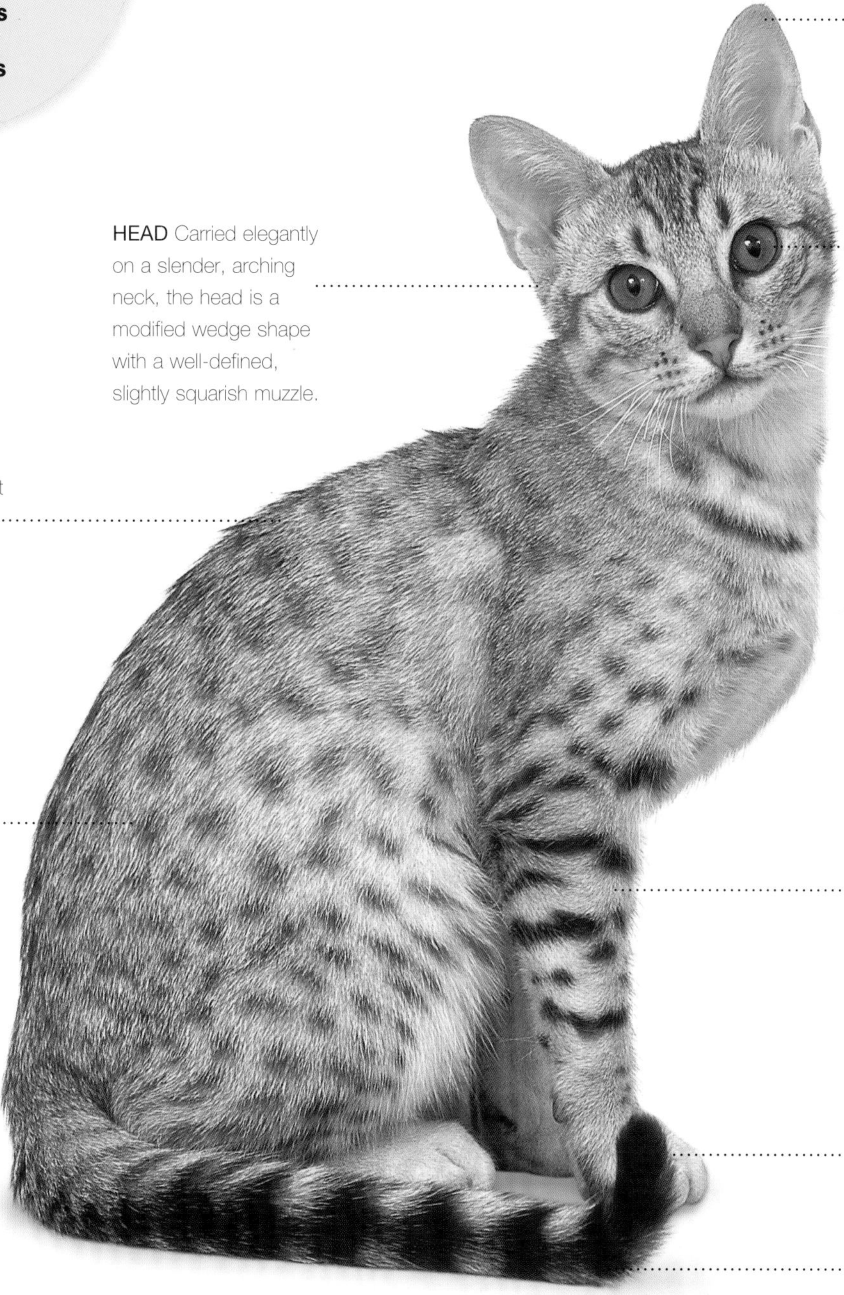

**EARS** Large ears with rounded tips and, sometimes, tufts of hair extending upward from the tips.

**HEAD** Carried elegantly on a slender, arching neck, the head is a modified wedge shape with a well-defined, slightly squarish muzzle.

**EYES** The eyes are large, expressive, and almond-shaped, and slanted. They may be any color except blue.

**COAT** Thick, satiny coat with a natural luster.

**COLOR** Round spots run in rows down the spine, with scattered spots over the sides and stomach. There are mascara markings round the eyes and a tabby "M" on the brow.

**LEGS** The legs are medium-long and well-muscled.

**PAWS** Compact, oval-shaped paws with pads that complement the coat coloring.

**TAIL** Long, slim tail with horizontal brush strokes. It tapers slightly to the dark tip.

# Bengal

## BENGAL FACTS

**PHYSIQUE** A medium to large cat with a long, sleek, muscular body.

**COAT** The brown Bengal comes in the spotted or marbled tabby pattern. There is also a snow variety, which has a pale background and a pattern that is much darker on the points than on the body.

**TEMPERAMENT** An alert, affectionate, and sociable cat. The Bengal is active and playful, and enjoys water.

**GROOMING** Regular stroking and occasional brushing is advised to keep the coat in good condition.

The Bengal is a hybrid breed, engineered by interbreeding domestic cats with the wild Asian Leopard Cat, which is native to the jungles and forests of southern Asia. It was developed by an American breeder, and came about partly as an offshoot of a scientific investigation into the nature of feline leukemia.

The Asian Leopard Cat is a wild animal, but in the 1950s these cats could be bought in pet shops in the United States. At this time, a female was acquired by a breeder named Jean Sugden. By chance, the cat mated with a black male, and produced a litter. One would expect these cats to be infertile, but, in the event, one of the female offspring was back-crossed, and produced some spotted offspring. These cats might have been used to found a new breed at the time, but Mrs Sugden's husband died and she abandoned the project. Almost 20 years later, Mrs Sugden—now Mrs Mill—heard of a breeding program involving Asian Leopard Cats that was being undertaken at the University of California. The project was aimed not at creating a new breed, but at finding out why the Asian Leopard Cat is partially immune to leukemia. Dr Willard Centerwall, who was conducting the research, donated some female hybrids to Jean Mill, who crossed them with (among others) non-pedigree cats and Egyptian Maus. Eventually, she succeeded in producing a domestic cat that showed the spotted and the marbled pattern of the wild beast. She called it the Bengal after the taxonomic designation of its Asian ancestor: Prionailurus bengalensis.

The Bengal excited much interest when it was registered in 1983—partly because the kittens were extremely expensive. Questions were also asked about its temperament: it was claimed that the Bengal's jungle nature could sometimes reassert itself. But Mrs Mill and other Bengal enthusiasts always insisted that any cat more than three generations removed from a wildcat (as they all now are) would be as gentle and domesticated as any other breed. The Bengal is now a popular breed in the UK, but it is not accepted by the American Cat Fanciers' Association, due to its hybrid origins.

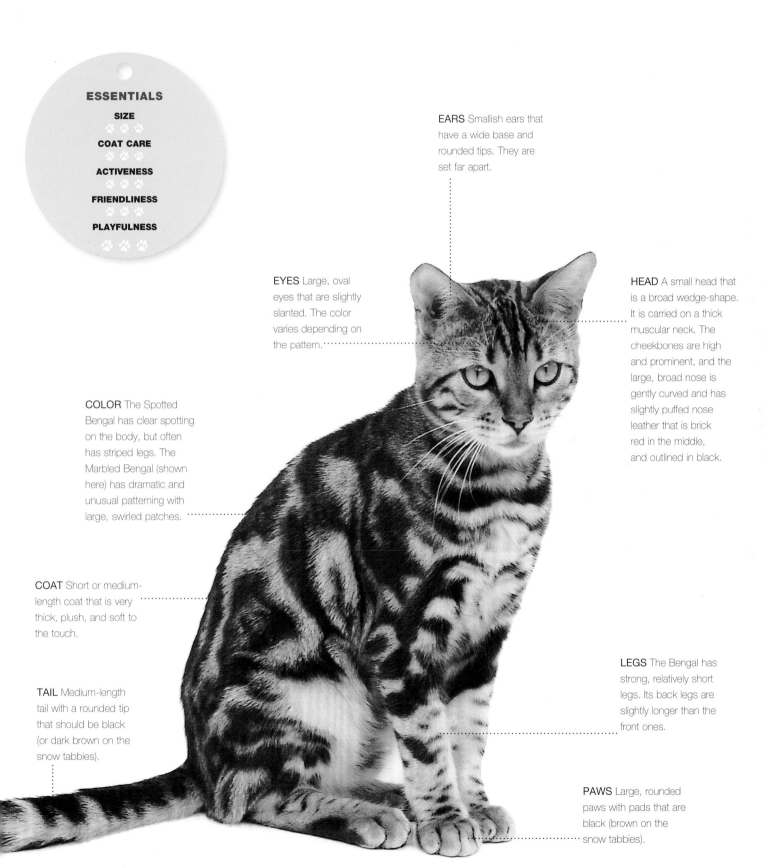

**ESSENTIALS**

**SIZE**

**COAT CARE**

**ACTIVENESS**

**FRIENDLINESS**

**PLAYFULNESS**

**EARS** Smallish ears that have a wide base and rounded tips. They are set far apart.

**EYES** Large, oval eyes that are slightly slanted. The color varies depending on the pattern.

**HEAD** A small head that is a broad wedge-shape. It is carried on a thick muscular neck. The cheekbones are high and prominent, and the large, broad nose is gently curved and has slightly puffed nose leather that is brick red in the middle, and outlined in black.

**COLOR** The Spotted Bengal has clear spotting on the body, but often has striped legs. The Marbled Bengal (shown here) has dramatic and unusual patterning with large, swirled patches.

**COAT** Short or medium-length coat that is very thick, plush, and soft to the touch.

**TAIL** Medium-length tail with a rounded tip that should be black (or dark brown on the snow tabbies).

**LEGS** The Bengal has strong, relatively short legs. Its back legs are slightly longer than the front ones.

**PAWS** Large, rounded paws with pads that are black (brown on the snow tabbies).

# Manx

## MANX FACTS

**PHYSIQUE** A compact cat with a rounded head, broad chest, short, arched back, and rounded rump. The hind legs are longer than the forelegs, making the Manx an excellent jumper.

**COAT** All colors and patterns except colorpointed are widely accepted. In the United States, ticked tabby, chocolate, and lavender Manx varieties are also not accepted.

**TEMPERAMENT** An even-tempered, active cat that enjoys lots of play. Most Manx are very loyal, with a tendency to bond with just one or two people.

**GROOMING** Frequent, gentle brushing will help to maintain the silkiness of the fur.

The lack of a tail makes the Manx one of the most recognizable breeds of cat. The breed is now so closely associated with the Isle of Man, its native habitat, that it has become the preeminent symbol of the island. Its rotund image regularly features on Manx postage stamps and commemorative coins.

Manx cats come in varying degrees of taillessness. Some have no tail at all, just a dimple at the base of the spine, and are known as "rumpies." Others have a residual tail, and are termed "risers" or "stumpies." Still others have an almost full-length tail: these are called "longies" or "tailies." There is a rare longhaired version called the Cymric (see p.144).

It is no coincidence that the few existing breeds of tailless cat arose on islands. The genetic mutation that creates this departure from the norm would die out if the cat population were not geographically restricted, and therefore inclined to inbreed. Unfortunately, the tailless gene can endow the Manx with fatal spinal problems: the offspring of two entirely tailless Manxes rarely survive kittenhood. For this reason, part or fully tailed cats are used in the breeding programs; only

the tailless cats are shown in the UK, although the American Cat Fanciers' Association accepts cats with a rumpy riser and FIFé recognizes the full range.

There are many legends telling how the Manx came to be without its tail. One says that the Manx was the last animal to enter Noah's Ark, because it insisted on hunting until the last possible moment. The Manx rushed up the gangplank of the ark just as it was setting sail. Its tail got caught in the slamming door, and was severed. A barely more plausible myth states that tailless cats sailed with the Spanish Armada of 1588, and were shipwrecked on the Isle of Man after the Spaniards were defeated.

Manxes are now bred on the Isle of Man to ensure that there is always a stock of this interesting cat in its homeland. The program is, one might say, a kind of government-sponsored "Noah's Ark" for the Manx alone.

**ESSENTIALS**

SIZE

COAT CARE

ACTIVENESS

FRIENDLINESS

PLAYFULNESS

**EARS** Widely spaced ears with a broad base and rounded tip. They are set high on the head and face slightly outward.

**EYES** Large, rounded, slightly slanted eyes. The eye color depends on the color of the coat.

**COAT** Short, dense, double coat with a slightly hard texture but glossy appearance. White Manx may have softer fur.

**HEAD** Rounded head with round cheeks and prominent jowls. The nose leather harmonizes with the color of the coat.

**TAIL** In the perfect Manx, there should be a rounded rump with no vestige of tail.

**LEGS** Sturdy legs that are longer behind than in front. This means that the rump is held higher than the shoulders.

**PAWS** Neat, rounded paws with pads that complement the color of the coat.

# Cymric

## CYMRIC FACTS

**PHYSIQUE** A solid, compact body with a broad chest and short, arched back that ends in a rounded rump. The completely tailless cat has a definite hollow where the tail should be, the "rumpie" has a residual bone, and the "stumpie" has a short tail.

**COAT** Most colors and patterns are accepted.

**TEMPERAMENT** A friendly, companionable, and playful cat that is an exceptional jumper.

**GROOMING** Frequent brushing is advised to keep the cat's coat in good condition.

The Cymric is simply a longhaired variant of the Manx cat, and some registries officially term it the "Longhaired Manx." The longhaired gene is present in the Manx lineage, so longhaired kittens sometimes occur. It was in Canada and the United States that breeders first used such kittens to create a new version of the famously tailless cat.

The name of the Cymric is a slightly Anglicized adaptation of the word cymraeg—which is Welsh for "Welsh". It was chosen because Wales is the closest country to the Isle of Man, native land of the Manx. It is a longstanding tradition among cat fanciers to give new breeds proximate geographical names if they are variants of breeds that have a strong link to a particular location. Precedents from other parts of the world include breeds such as the Balinese (Bali is close to ancient Siam, supposed origin of the Siamese) and the Somali (Somalia borders Ethiopia, historic homeland of the Abyssinian).

As for the Cymric, it is an entirely North American cat. The work to fix the longhaired gene was done in the 1960s by two breeders—Blair Wright in Canada and Leslie Falteseik in the United States.

The cat was recognized by the Canadian Cat Association in 1970, and by the American Cat Fanciers' Association (CFA) in 1989. The CFA at first approved the name Cymric, but now favours Longhaired Manx. The cat is not recognized at all in Europe or in Britain, where it is, in any case, almost unknown.

Apart from the length of its coat, the Cymric is in every way identical to the Manx original. The cat can be a "longie" or a "stumpie"—that is, with some vestige of a tail—or it can be an entirely tailless "rumpie." It has the same long hind legs as the Manx, and so walks with the characteristic hopping gate. Since the gene that produces taillessness is related to the defect that leads to spina bifida, the Cymric, like the Manx, is prone to potentially fatal spinal problems if breeders concentrate too single-mindedly on propagating those completely without a tail.

**EARS** Set high on the head and widely spaced, the ears have a broad base and a rounded tip.

**EYES** The eyes are large, round, and slightly slanted. The color varies depending on the color of the coat.

**COAT** Medium-length double coat that is longer at the rump and abdomen, and has a ruff at the front and full britches. The texture is soft and silky.

**ESSENTIALS**

**SIZE**

**COAT CARE**

**ACTIVENESS**

**FRIENDLINESS**

**PLAYFULNESS**

**TAIL** In the perfect Cymric, there should be a rounded rump with no vestige of tail.

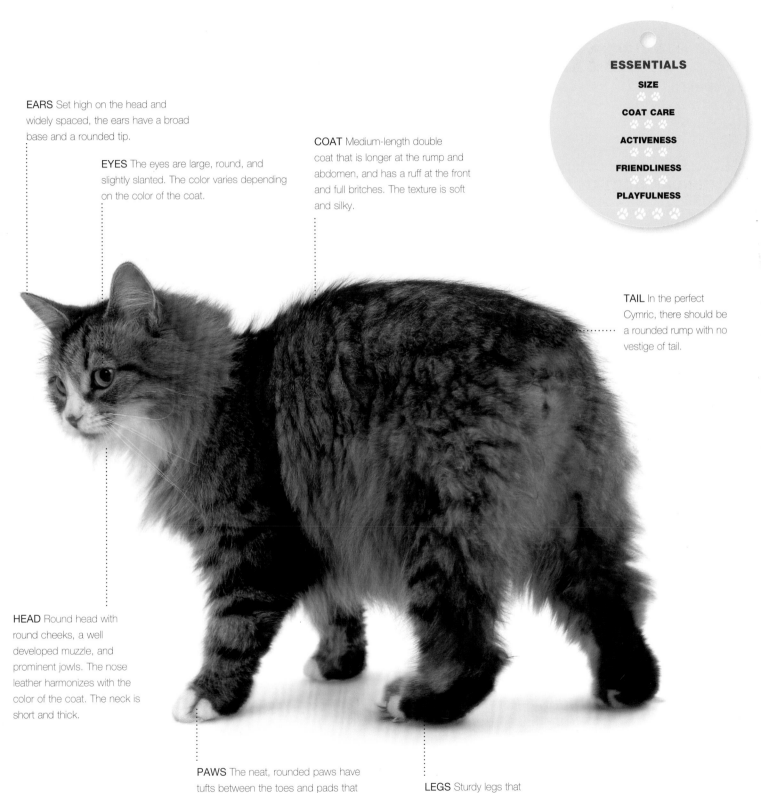

**HEAD** Round head with round cheeks, a well developed muzzle, and prominent jowls. The nose leather harmonizes with the color of the coat. The neck is short and thick.

**PAWS** The neat, rounded paws have tufts between the toes and pads that complement the color of the coat.

**LEGS** Sturdy legs that are longer behind than in front.

# American Bobtail

## AMERICAN BOBTAIL FACTS

**PHYSIQUE** An athletic, medium-large cat with a long body and broad chest. Its long sturdy legs and good musculature help to give it a naturally wild appearance. Its tail should measure 1–4 in (2.5–10 cm) in length.

**COAT** All colors and patterns are recognized.

**TEMPERAMENT** An agreeable and adaptable cat that makes a loyal family pet. The American Bobtail can live happily with most dogs. It is easy to train and can make a good traveller if it starts young.

**GROOMING** Only occasional brushing is required to maintain the coat, which is non-matting.

*Most short-tailed cats are island breeds, like the Manx and the Japanese Bobtails. The American Bobtail is an exception—a short-tailed mutation that occurred naturally in the United States, and just happened to be noticed at the right moment. It is one of the few breeds that can truly call itself "all-American."*

The term American Bobtail has been applied to several different breeds, but the officially recognized bearers of the name are all descended from a short-tailed stray tabby named Yodie, spotted on a Native American Reservation in Arizona by John and Brenda Sanders. They were on vacation in Arizona, and at the end of their stay they took the homeless, tailless male cat back home with them to Iowa, where it mated with their Siamese.

Some of the resulting kittens were short-tailed like their father. The next generation produced a litter in which all the kittens were short-tailed. These were crossed with Himalayans to produce the short-tailed, thick-coated cats that are the founding stock of the breed. A friend of the Sanders family christened the breed American Bobtail, but some confusion surrounds this name. Elsewhere in America, there were reports of breeders producing short-tailed cats—also termed American Bobtails—by crossing domestic varieties with the bobcat, a wild form of lynx that is native to North America. The reports seemed unlikely, but they have never been conclusively disproved. Even if such hybrids had been successfully produced, they would most probably be infertile, and so would constitute the first and last generation of their kind.

So, for all practical purposes, it is Yodie's descendants who are the true American Bobtails. The cat now exists in both shorthaired and longhaired versions. Although the shorthairs came first, it is the longhairs, which have a large ruff like that of a wild bobcat, that most resemble their ancestor Yodie. American Bobtails are extremely agreeable cats but, inexplicably, they have a kleptomanic fondness for bright, shiny objects. They steal such things without compunction, so owners of American Bobtails soon learn to keep their jewellry and silverware safely locked away.

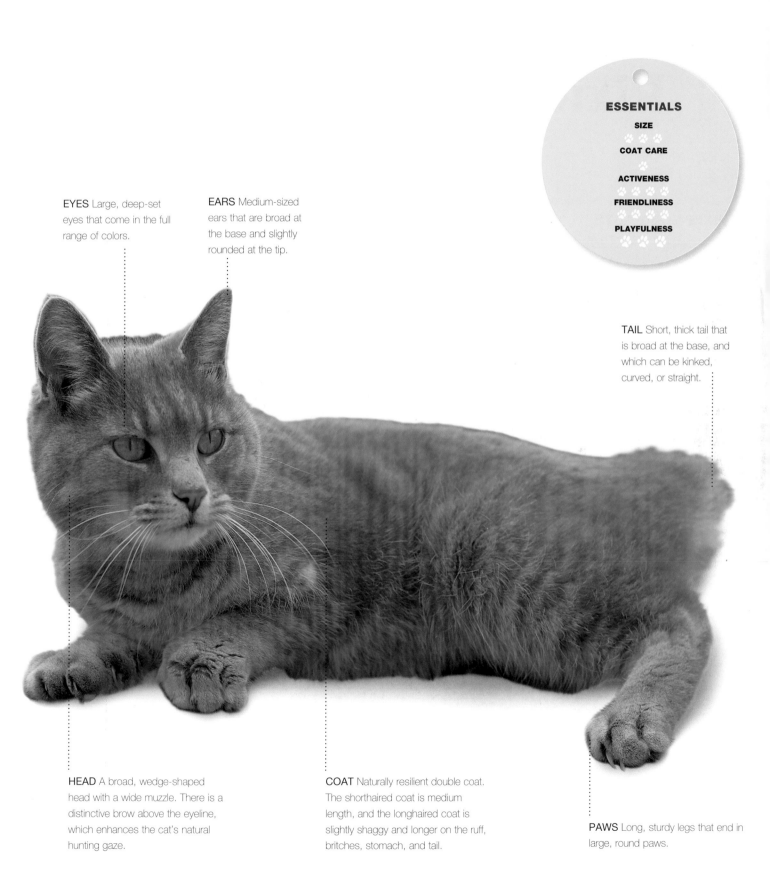

**ESSENTIALS**
SIZE
COAT CARE
ACTIVENESS
FRIENDLINESS
PLAYFULNESS

**EYES** Large, deep-set eyes that come in the full range of colors.

**EARS** Medium-sized ears that are broad at the base and slightly rounded at the tip.

**TAIL** Short, thick tail that is broad at the base, and which can be kinked, curved, or straight.

**HEAD** A broad, wedge-shaped head with a wide muzzle. There is a distinctive brow above the eyeline, which enhances the cat's natural hunting gaze.

**COAT** Naturally resilient double coat. The shorthaired coat is medium length, and the longhaired coat is slightly shaggy and longer on the ruff, britches, stomach, and tail.

**PAWS** Long, sturdy legs that end in large, round paws.

# Pixie Bob

## PIXIE BOB FACTS

**PHYSIQUE** A large, muscular, heavy-boned cat that is broad in the chest and has long, sturdy legs with large paws. It may have up to seven toes on each foot—the only breed where this is allowed.

**COAT** The Pixie Bob is a brown spotted tabby. There are no varieties.

**TEMPERAMENT** Loving and tractable by nature, this is a quiet, undemanding cat.

**GROOMING** Regular brushing will help to maintain the appearance of the coat and prevent matting in the longhaired version.

The Pixie Bob is bred to resemble The North American Bobcat. With its wild face, bobtail, spotted coat, polydactyl feet and large size, it is an impressive sight. There is something distinctly magical about Pixie Bobs. The "wild" look, their increased "sway" and larger size all add up to make it a unique breed with an intriguing history.

The Pixie Bob's life began in 1985 by breed founder Carol Ann Brewer. It is alleged that a natural mating took place between a Coastal Red Bobcat and a polydactyl barn cat, with a polydactyl male—named "Legend Cat"—purchased from the resulting litter. Intrigued by this kitten's appearance and unusual behaviour, within a year Carol had purchased another cat with the same kind of heritage, as well as a cat from an unknown heritage but with the same build, tail and traits. A female from a mating of two of the original cats was called Pixie, hence the name Pixie Bob. The Pixie Bob was TICA (the International Cat Association) registered in 1995 as "a new breed and colour" and in 1997 for Championship status, having been DNA tested for wild markings and found to be carrying none. Thanks to the UK's Alsoomse Pixie Bobs cattery, they are causing quite a stir in homes and in TICA show rings. When Pixie Bobs walk they "sway" or swagger. They have big shoulders

and prominent shoulder blades, producing a rolling gait. There is a dip behind the shoulders that inclines slightly towards the hips, which are slightly higher than the shoulder; the hip and shoulder angles are also straighter than that of other breeds. With longer legs at the back, they are a muscular cat with heavy boning; males can be 12–25 lbs and females 8–15 lbs.

The Pixie Bobs temperament is outstanding. They are very loving and loyal, playful with out being hyperactive, and are very sharp, intelligent and quick to learn. They are amazing companions that get on well with other animals – cats and dogs alike – and are very gentle with children, often treating them like another sibling. They do have some "dog" characteristics and will follow you around, chatting and giving little clicks to let you know they are there. They are known to greet you with a wagging tail and will bond very strongly with family members. They even enjoy walks on the lead and rides in the car!

**ESSENTIALS**

SIZE

COAT CARE

ACTIVENESS

FRIENDLINESS

PLAYFULNESS

**EARS** Wide at the base and medium in size, the ears have rounded tips, sometimes with small tufts of hair, and are set slightly to the side of the head.

**HEAD** Medium to large pear-shaped head with heavily hooded eyes. The nose is wide and brick in color and the large muzzle has a strong fleshy chin, giving a "pout".

**EYES** Medium-sized triangular-shaped eyes that are dark rimmed. The only accepted colors are gold/hazel and gooseberry green.

**COAT** Short, woolly coat that stands away from the body in the shorthaired version; medium-long, soft and closer-lying in the longhaired version. The hair is longer on the stomach in both types, and there is heavy hair over the eyes.

**TAIL** This can be non-existent to 5 inches or longer in length. Kinks and knots are acceptable.

**COLOR** Randomly spotted coat in light to medium brown.

**LEGS** Long, heavy-boned, muscular legs.

**PAWS** Large, wide, rounded paws, with up to seven toes on each paw. The pads are dark brown or black.

# Japanese Bobtail

## JAPANESE BOBTAIL FACTS

🐾 **PHYSIQUE** This is a medium-sized, lean cat with a long, slim body and a triangular head. The hind legs are longer than the forelegs.

🐾 **COAT** The Japanese Bobtail is recognized in most colors and patterns, except pointed and ticked tabby.

🐾 **TEMPERAMENT** An affectionate and inquisitive cat that makes a loving pet. It needs plenty of attention and play to prevent it from becoming bored. The Japanese Bobtail can be highly vocal—some owners say that it "sings."

🐾 **GROOMING** Light, daily brushing is recommended.

The Japanese Bobtail is known in Japan as mi-ke, the "three-fur cat." The most prized type is white with prominent patches of black and red. The residual tail is longer than it looks, but is tightly curled and so resembles a powder puff. This is considered a lucky trait in Japan, where long-tailed cats are associated with devils and changelings.

The Japanese Bobtail is a naturally occurring breed that was once found all over southeast Asia. The bobbed tail became a fixed feature only when the cat came to Japan. The island environment served to restrict the cat's gene pool, and so gave its short "bunny-rabbit" tail a much better chance of being transmitted from one generation to the next.

Yet the Bobtail, though not a native Japanese animal, has certainly been in Japan for a very long time—at least a thousand years if the evidence of ancient Japanese art and literature is to be believed. It has been suggested that the Bobtail was introduced to Japan from China in the 10th century, during the reign of Emperor Ichijo. He is known to have loved cats, and it is said that he made a law that they must not work. Unfortunately, this decision allowed mice to run amok and destroy the silkworms on which Japan's silk industry depended. So the Emperor reversed his decree, and declared that all cats must hunt. The pampered Bobtails became street cats, and were known as kazuko neko—family cats. They can still be seen running free in Japanese cities.

Some Bobtails raise a paw when seated, and this has led them to be associated with the maneki-neko, the beckoning cat of Japanese myth. The gesture is believed to bring good luck. Prints and porcelain models of the beckoning cat are to be found in many Japanese homes, and usually they bear the markings of the Japanese Bobtail. Certainly this is a personable, hospitable cat. It is now once again common outside its Japanese homeland, and had been bred in the United States since the 1960s.

**ESSENTIALS**

SIZE

COAT CARE

ACTIVENESS

FRIENDLINESS

PLAYFULNESS

**COLOR** The Japanese Bobtail can be any color, but should ideally have bold dramatic markings.

**COAT** Soft, medium-length coat with a silky texture. Longhaired cats have a ruff at the front.

**TAIL** Short tail measuring no more than 3 in (7.5 cm) that can be curled or straight. The tail hair is fanned, like a powder puff.

**EARS** The large, upright ears have round tips and are set wide apart. The longhaired cat should have tufts on the ears.

**EYES** Large, oval-shaped eyes set at a slant toward the ears. The color depends on the coloring of the coat.

**HEAD** An almost perfect equilateral triangle, the head has prominent cheekbones, a broad muzzle, and a long nose. The nose leather harmonizes with the color of the coat.

**LEGS** The legs are long and slender without being delicate.

**PAWS** Medium-sized, egg-shaped paws with pads that complement the color of the coat. In longhaired cats, the paws are tufted.

# Scottish Fold

## SCOTTISH FOLD FACTS

**PHYSIQUE** Medium-sized cat with rounded, "cobby" body and short, sturdy legs

**COAT** Most colors and patterns are accepted.

**TEMPERAMENT** Placid and adaptable cat that is sociable and generally sweet-tempered. It generally gets on well with children and dogs. A good mouser, the Scottish Fold enjoys spending time outdoors.

**GROOMING** Regular brushing is needed to maintain the coat. The ears should be checked regularly.

The Scottish Fold is a breed of cat with ears that lie flat on its head. This peculiarity gives its face an appealingly human appearance: it looks like a 1920s dandy, with hair parted down the middle. The breed came about in the 1960s, and is descended from a Scottish farm cat.

The first Scottish Fold was born on a farm near the village of Coupar Angus, 13 miles from the Scottish city of Perth. She was a white female, one of a litter of cats with perfectly normal ears. It seems certain that the gene that produces the folded ear is a spontaneous natural mutation.

The white cat with the strange ears was named Susie. In 1963 she gave birth to a litter of four, two of which had the folded ear. One of these—a female as white as her mother—was given to a local shepherd named William Ross. He and his wife Mary were interested in cat breeding, and they saw that the new cat, which they named Snooks, might form the basis of a new breed. This they tentatively called the "Lop-Eared Cat."

In 1967, one of Snooks's immediate descendants, a male called Snowdrift, was given to a professional breeder in London named Pat Turner. She developed the breed and came up with the name Scottish Fold: the cat's ears, were, after all, nothing like the floppy ears of a rabbit. Turner introduced the new breed to the cat-breeding community, but her efforts were condemned by many authorities, which saw the folded ear as a deformity that could cause health problems, and so should not be encouraged. It also transpired that the fold gene could lead to skeletal deformities if two Folds mate.

For these reasons, British associations declined to register the breed. But some Scottish Folds were exported to the United States, where the breed was registered in 1973. Selective breeding has produced a tighter ear-fold that lays closer to the head than was the case with the founding stock.

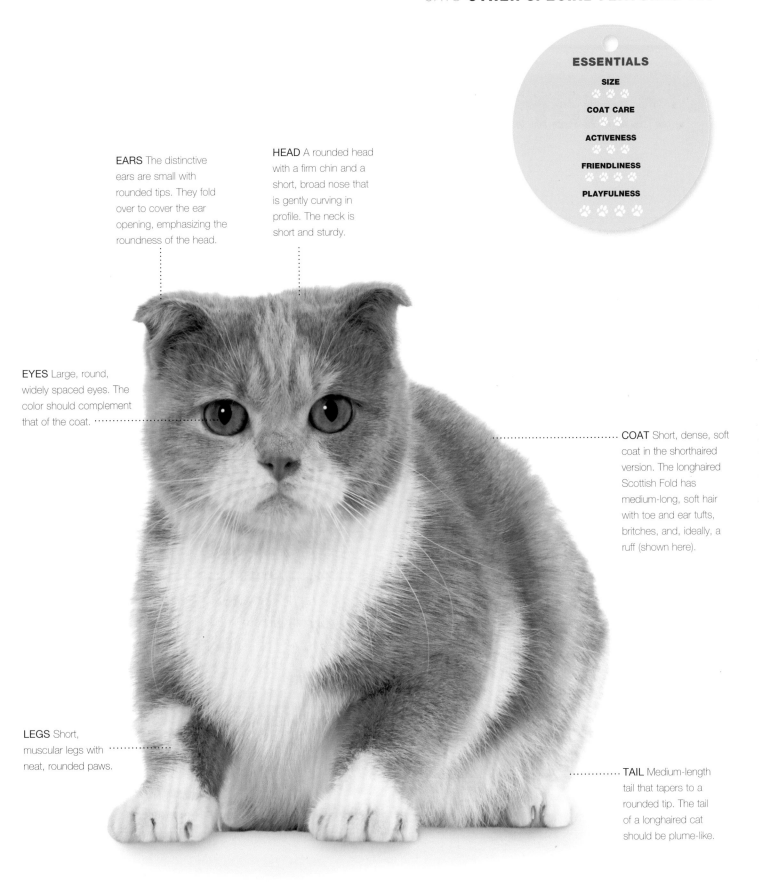

**ESSENTIALS**

SIZE

COAT CARE

ACTIVENESS

FRIENDLINESS

PLAYFULNESS

**EARS** The distinctive ears are small with rounded tips. They fold over to cover the ear opening, emphasizing the roundness of the head.

**HEAD** A rounded head with a firm chin and a short, broad nose that is gently curving in profile. The neck is short and sturdy.

**EYES** Large, round, widely spaced eyes. The color should complement that of the coat.

**COAT** Short, dense, soft coat in the shorthaired version. The longhaired Scottish Fold has medium-long, soft hair with toe and ear tufts, britches, and, ideally, a ruff (shown here).

**LEGS** Short, muscular legs with neat, rounded paws.

**TAIL** Medium-length tail that tapers to a rounded tip. The tail of a longhaired cat should be plume-like.

# American Curl

## AMERICAN CURL FACTS

**PHYSIQUE** A medium-sized, slender, and elegant cat with good musculature.

**COAT** All colors and patterns are accepted.

**TEMPERAMENT** American Curls exhibit a kittenlike tendency for play in adulthood. They are remarkably friendly and affectionate, and highly inquisitive. American Curls are tolerant, adaptable cats, and can get along well with children as well as other animals, including dogs.

**GROOMING** Occasional brushing is all that is needed to keep the coat in good condition.

The defining feature of the American Curl cat is the extraordinary shape of its ears. They curl backward, as if the cat were facing into a high wind—or we might say that they are fluted like a seashell. This physical peculiarity is combined with the sweetest of feline temperaments, making the playful and adaptable American Curl an ideal companion.

The American Curl, like so many of the newer breeds, came about as the result of a spontaneous genetic mutation in the general cat population. The first of the kind was a black, longhaired stray cat that presented itself on the doorstep of John and Grace Ruga of Lakewood, California, in 1981. The Rugas noticed her strange ears right away, and decided to keep her. They named her Shulamith, after the "black and comely" princess in the biblical Song of Solomon. Within six months, Shulamith had given birth to a litter, two of which sported her curled ears. All three cats were exhibited in Palm Springs in 1983, and the breed became established in the United States very quickly after that. The American Curl was accepted by The International Cat Association in 1985, and by the Cat Fanciers' Association in 1986.

All American Curls are born with perfectly normal, straight ears. They begin to curl during the first week of life, and soon each ear resembles a tightly wound rosebud on the cat's head. The ears then slowly unfurl before reaching a fixed state at about four months. Some American Curls are curlier in the ear than others, and for show purposes, the greater the degree of curl, the better. The ideal American Curl has ears that form a smooth arc.

The first American Curls were longhairs, which boasted a luxuriant plumed tail. Further breeding programs have produced a shorthaired American Curl, but this was hard to achieve since so many shorthaired curls carry the longhaired gene. Today, shorthaired American Curls remain rare. All American Curls, shorthaired or long, share the same whimsical, affectionate personality.

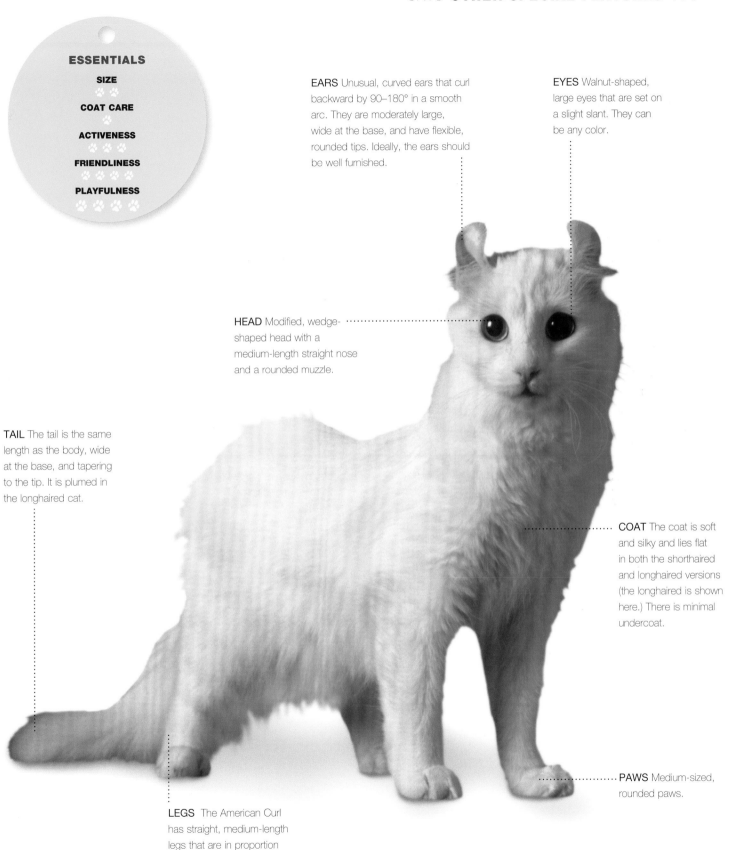

**ESSENTIALS**

SIZE

COAT CARE

ACTIVENESS

FRIENDLINESS

PLAYFULNESS

**EARS** Unusual, curved ears that curl backward by 90–180° in a smooth arc. They are moderately large, wide at the base, and have flexible, rounded tips. Ideally, the ears should be well furnished.

**EYES** Walnut-shaped, large eyes that are set on a slight slant. They can be any color.

**HEAD** Modified, wedge-shaped head with a medium-length straight nose and a rounded muzzle.

**TAIL** The tail is the same length as the body, wide at the base, and tapering to the tip. It is plumed in the longhaired cat.

**COAT** The coat is soft and silky and lies flat in both the shorthaired and longhaired versions (the longhaired is shown here.) There is minimal undercoat.

**PAWS** Medium-sized, rounded paws.

**LEGS** The American Curl has straight, medium-length legs that are in proportion with the body.

# Munchkin

## MUNCHKIN FACTS

🐾 **PHYSIQUE** Medium-sized, muscular body with well-rounded chest. The legs are short, but well-muscled, and are longer at the back than the front.

🐾 **COAT** All colors and patterns are accepted.

🐾 **TEMPERAMENT** An outgoing and inquisitive cat that has a kittenlike sense of play. Munchkins are said to be tolerant of other animals and of children.

🐾 **GROOMING** Occasional brushing is all that is necessary for the shorthaired varieties. Longhaired Munchkins need regular grooming to maintain the coat.

The Munchkin is in many ways a very ordinary cat. Its only distinguishing feature is its startlingly short legs. But this characteristic has made it one of the most controversial breeds. Many cat fanciers and some authorities feel that its stunted form constitutes a freakish departure from the feline norm, and so should not be encouraged.

As with many of the newer breeds of cat, the Munchkin owes its origin to a random genetic mutation that survived only as a result of human intervention. In 1983, a breeder named Sandra Hochenedel found a black street cat under a truck in the town of Rayville, Louisiana. The cat, which she named Blackberry, had very short legs and was pregnant. Some of the subsequent litter also had short legs—and so provided ready material for a breeding program designed to perpetuate the mutation. The new breed was very quickly dubbed the Munchkin—after the diminutive people in the Wizard of Oz movie. The cat is also sometimes called the Dachshund Cat (by analogy with the short-legged terrier) or the Minikat. The shortest Munchkins are known graphically as "rug-huggers." But jolly nomenclature notwithstanding, the Munchkin caused uproar in the cat world. Many experts worried that it would be prone to the same spinal problems as short-legged dogs; others objected on aesthetic grounds that the Munchkin was a cat that had been deliberately deprived of a cat's innately graceful proportions.

Proponents of the breed deny that there are health problems connected with the Munchkin's strange shape; they say that cats' spines are naturally more flexible than dogs', and that this averts any tendency towards back problems. As for the aesthetic argument, fans of the Munchkin point to its gentle nature, its appealing habit of standing on its hind legs like a squirrel, and its surprising athleticism.

Breeders have succeeded in producing Munchkins in both shorthaired and longhaired varieties, and in every conceivable variety of coat color and pattern (there is even a rexed variant called a Skookum). But most registries have declined to acknowledge this unusual cat.

**ESSENTIALS**

SIZE

COAT CARE

ACTIVENESS

FRIENDLINESS

PLAYFULNESS

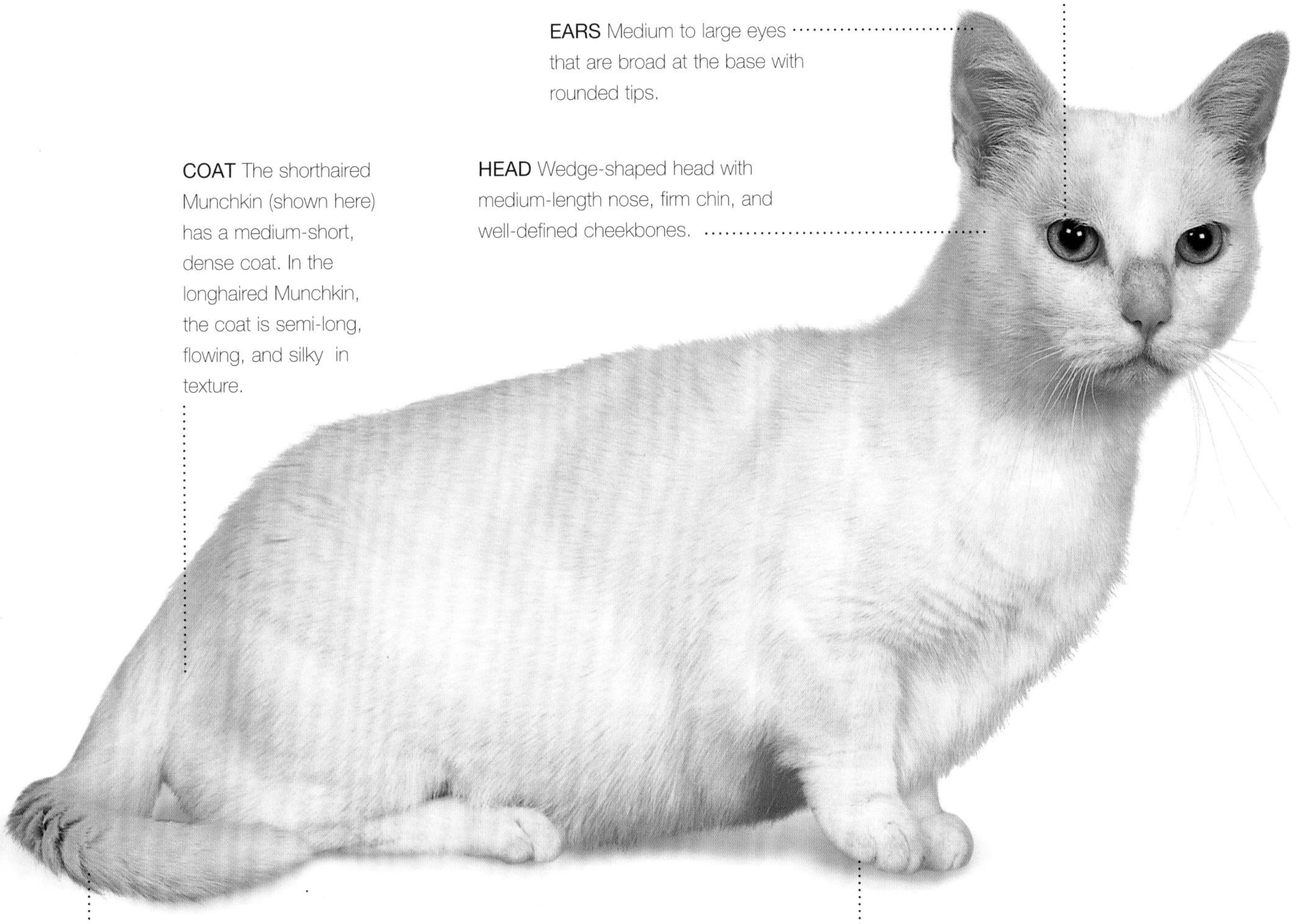

**EYES** Wide-spaced, walnut-shaped eyes that are slightly angled toward the ears. They can be any color.

**EARS** Medium to large eyes that are broad at the base with rounded tips.

**COAT** The shorthaired Munchkin (shown here) has a medium-short, dense coat. In the longhaired Munchkin, the coat is semi-long, flowing, and silky in texture.

**HEAD** Wedge-shaped head with medium-length nose, firm chin, and well-defined cheekbones.

**TAIL** Long tail that reaches the shoulders if laid along the back. It tapers to a rounded tip, and is generally carried high off the ground.

**LEGS** Short, sturdy legs, with the hindl egs being slightly longer than the forelegs. The paws are rounded.

# Sphynx

## SPHYNX FACTS

**PHYSIQUE** A medium-sized, broad-chested cat. The legs are well-muscled and medium in length, with the back legs being slightly longer than the front ones.

**COAT** All colors and patterns are accepted.

**TEMPERAMENT** A very lively, playful cat. The Sphynx generally has a sweet disposition and enjoys being petted.

**GROOMING** The Sphynx needs regular washing to remove oil on the skin. It benefits from a daily rubbing-down with a chamois-type cloth. It is vulnerable to sunstroke, so belongs indoors.

No breed of cat elicits a stronger response than the furless Sphynx, which originated in Canada as the result of a genetic mutation. "The ugliest cat in the world" is one of the more mild epithets to have been applied to this extraordinary animal. Although almost completely bald, the Sphynx comes in all the colors and patterns of more hirsute breeds.

Hairless cats have been around for centuries but the Sphynx that we see today began to be developed in the 1970's. Extensive breeding over the years has developed a strong and healthy breed that, although unusual, is a wide source of interest.

The skin of the Sphynx has a tough, suede-like texture that feels warm to the touch. The color of the skin varies and comes in several patterns – the color of the skin is the color that the fur would have been. Although there is no coat to speak of that needs maintaining, the lack of fur can cause problems for the Sphynx and requires some care. Body oils that are usually absorbed in a cat's fur can build up on the Sphynx, but a regular bath – once a week should suffice – is enough to prevent this from causing problems.

Like humans, Sphynx skin can burn in sunlight so it is important to keep a close eye on the cat when it is let outside. It is advisable to always accompany this breed outdoors and only allow limited exposure to the sun.

Despite its wrinkled and odd appearance, the Sphynx is an extremely affectionate cat that likes to cuddle up to its owner – sometimes in an attempt to keep warm! This cat likes attention and is not very reserved; a sense of humour is required with this lively cat who can behave like a clown for attention. Acrobatic and energetic, the Sphynx is a show off who is guaranteed to make you laugh. Known to be an extrovert, these cats do well in a showing environment.

**ESSENTIALS**

**SIZE**
❀ ❀ ❀

**COAT CARE**
❀ ❀ ❀

**ACTIVENESS**
❀ ❀

**FRIENDLINESS**
❀ ❀ ❀

**PLAYFULNESS**
❀ ❀ ❀

**EYES** Large, rounded eyes that are slightly slanted.

**HEAD** Wedge-shaped with prominent cheekbones and a flattish forehead. Short nose with leather that complements the coat color. Whiskers may be absent.

**EARS** The ears are very large and open, with broad bases. There may be wisps of hair on the outsides, but the insides are hairless.

**TAIL** Slender, whiplike tail that tapers to a narrow tip. There may be a small "puff" of hair on the tip.

**COAT** Although it appears hairless, the Sphynx may be covered in a short, fine down. The skin is wrinkled, warm to the touch, with the feel of chamois leather.

**PAWS** The paws are egg-shaped, with prominent, long, and slender toes. The paw pads are thicker than usual.

# Peterbald

## PETERBALD FACTS

**PHYSIQUE** Medium-sized cat with a long, elongated body.

**COAT** All colors and all patterns are accepted.

**TEMPERAMENT** An affectionate, indoor cat that needs plenty of attention and which can be demanding. It is playful, inquisitive, and very outgoing. The Peterbald is tolerant of children.

**GROOMING** Unlike the Sphynx, the Peterbald produces little oil on the skin. It needs only the occasional bath to keep it healthy.

The Peterbald was developed in Russia in the 1990s. Although hairless, the Peterbald has no connection to the Sphynx and is the result of an entirely different genetic mutation. It can be entirely bald, be covered in a fuzzy down, or have a sparse, curly coat called a "brush" coat. Unlike the Sphynx, it has curly or kinked whiskers.

The Peterbald is described as being a very elegant and graceful cat, with a muscular build and long legs. In fact, everything about this cat seems to be long; the legs, the body, the tail and the neck are all extended and highlighted by the lack of fur. It was recognized by The International Cat Association in 1997, and the World Cat Federation in 2003, and made championship status in 2005 by TICA.

Like the Sphynx, the Peterbald needs regular grooming to ensure that the oil levels on the skin are balanced, so a weekly bath is recommended to keep the skin from developing ailments. Pay attention to the ears and nails also, as these are hotspots for problems caused by lack of hair. The Peterbald is susceptible to burning in sunlight, so ensure that this breed has limited exposure to the sunlight and keep an eye on it outside.

It is worth noting that hairless cats are not necessarily the answer for those with allergies to cats and fur, as the oils produced by the skin may trigger a reaction. Be sure to spend time with Peterbalds before taking one home, and do the relevant research if you'd like one as a pet.

This entertaining breed is energetic and acrobatic, and will make you laugh with its antics. The Peterbald is playful and likes to spend time with its owner, but will make his own games too. An inquisitive chap, this cat likes to investigate and can get itself into all sorts of situations. A wonderful pet, this breed is happy with other pets, people and children but they shouldn't be left alone for prolonged periods of time.

**HEAD** An elongated triangle in shape, set on a long, slender neck. The muzzle is narrow and the tip forms a straight line with the tip of the nose, which is long and straight. There may be whiskers, which are crinkly, kinked, or broken.

**ESSENTIALS**

SIZE

COAT CARE

ACTIVENESS

FRIENDLINESS

PLAYFULNESS

**EYES** Almond-shaped eyes that are set in a slight slant. They can be of any color .

**EARS** Extremely large, pointed ears that are wide at the base.

**COAT** The hairless Peterbald (shown here) has a soft, wrinkled skin with a texture akin to suede. The cat also may be covered in a soft down, or have a "brush coat."

**LEGS** The Peterbald has long, slim legs. The hind legs are slightly longer than the forelegs.

**PAWS** Medium-sized, oval paws with long, prominent toes.

**TAIL** Long, whiplike tail that tapers to a fine point.

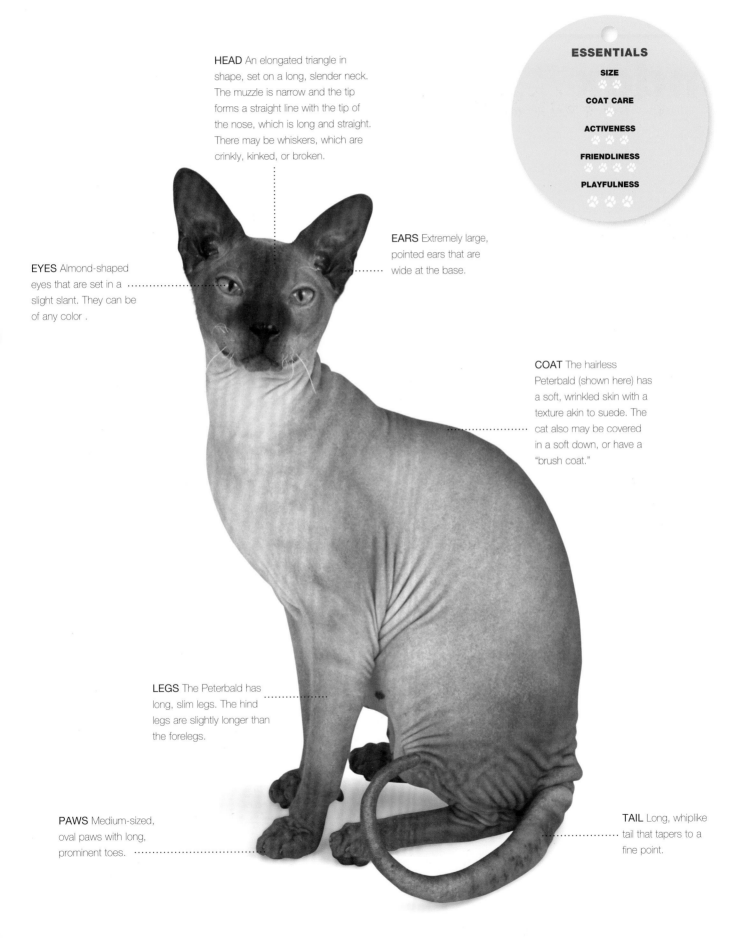

# Index